CHICAGO PUBLIC LIBRARY
HAROLD WASHINGTON LIBRARY CENTER

R0042496912

FORM 125 M

EDUCATION & PHILOSOPHY

The Chicago Public Library

MAR 20 1985

Received

A Handbook for School District Financial Management

By *Dr. Frederick L. Dembowski*

Published by the Research Corporation of the
Association of School Business Officials
of the United States and Canada
720 Garden Street, Park Ridge, IL 60068
312/823-9320

COPYRIGHT 1982 BY THE

RESEARCH CORPORATION

OF THE

ASSOCIATION OF SCHOOL BUSINESS OFFICIALS

An educational research organization
incorporated not for profit

All Rights Reserved Under International
and Pan American Copyright Conventions

International Standard Book No.: 0-910170-24-X

Printed in U.S.A.

To order additional copies of this publication, contact:
Publications Dept., Research Corp. of the
Association of School Business Officials
of the United States and Canada
720 Garden Street, Park Ridge, IL 60068
(312) 823-9320

Comments in this publication may be divergent in point of view and controversial in nature. The materials published herein, and the comments made, represent the ideas, beliefs or opinions of the authors and are not necessarily the views or policies of the Research Corporation of the Association of School Business Officials of the United States and Canada and/or the Association of School Business Officials of the United States and Canada.

TABLE OF CONTENTS

Preface..iv

Acknowledgements...vi

Introduction..vii

Section I -- An Overview of
   School District Financial Management Operations...................1

Section II -- Financial Management Practices......................39

Section III -- State-by-State Summaries of
   School District Financial Management Practices..................59

Section IV -- An Annotated Bibliography..........................111

Appendix A -- Sample Questionnaire,
   School District Cash Management Survey........................119

PREFACE

The basic, underlying professional objective of the Research Corporation of the Association of School Business Officials (RC-ASBO) is to identify and share timely, appropriate information about successful school business management practices.

ASBO's Research Corporation is an integral part of the Association's activities. As a publishing/research subsidiary, it is devoted to advancing educational management at all levels by conducting and promoting significant research programs staffed with hundreds of "expert" generalists and specialists who continually confront the most pressing issues facing educators, educational administration and school business management.

This Handbook for School District Financial Management is another example of how RC-ASBO programs meet the objectives listed above.

International ASBO often works with other associations and organizations in developing publications and conducting research, particularly its affiliated state/provincial Associations of School Business Officials. This publication is such a joint project and was developed in cooperation with the New York State Association of School Business Officials (NYSASBO). In 1981, the NYSASBO published a book entitled "A Handbook of School Banking Relations." That publication, also written by Dr. Dembowski, focused on school/banking relations in the state of New York and served as the basis for developing this publication.

This project, including the accompanying research that led to the publication of this handbook, was initiated because the area of school district financial management is one of the fastest growing concerns to school business officials. Financial management in school districts has become increasingly important over the past several years because of declining enrollments, reduced state/provincial/federal funding, tight budgets, school closings and a plathora of related influences that are putting constant pressures on public school systems in the United States and Canada to "do more with less".

One way in which school districts can meet these challenges and stretch their available financial resources -- while generating additional revenues -- is through an effective and efficient financial management system that insures adequate cash availability to meet daily needs and a maximum return on the investment of idle funds. With large amounts of revenue at stake, it is no wonder that cash management is now recognized as an increasingly important function in school business management.

This publication is intended to provide information and guidelines on how school districts can initiate an effective and efficient cash management system or improve their existing cash management systems.

Charles G. Stolberg
Associate Executive Director - Research Services

ACKNOWLEDGEMENTS

This publication provides an introduction to the terminology, concepts and practices of school district cash management, investing, borrowing and banking. While many of the more innovative and advanced techniques have been purposely left out of this Handbook, the Annotated Bibliography will provide guidance to readers seeking that type of information.

This Handbook is divided into four sections. The first presents an overview of school district financial management and acquaints the reader with the topic. Section two presents a discussion of the responses to a 1980 survey of school district cash management practices in each of the 50 states. This section compares and contrasts what various states can and cannot do, and, hopefully, will provide the stimulus for an analysis of the legislation governing cash management in the 50 states. The next section contains a state-by-state summary of cash management practices in each of the 50 states. The final section presents an Annotated Bibliography of other literature concerning school district financial management for those readers who wish to explore the topic in greater detail.

Thanks are due to a number of people who contributed to the completion and success of this project. Dr. Bruce Brummitt, the Executive Director of New York State ASBO, and Charles Stolberg of International ASBO, provided the impetus for this project. Section I was written with the help of Mr. Robert Davey of Chemical Bank in Albany, New York. Ms. Janice Biros, my able graduate assistant, provided much of the "legwork" in organizing the workflow. Other persons involved in completing the project include Dr. Sidney Decker, Fred Goodman and Marilyn Van Dyke, all of SUNY Albany. Of course, my thanks go to those professionals in the 50 states who responded to our survey. Finally, sincere thanks go to Barbara Grubalski and Karen Ceresia who did the hardest job, the typing.

This Handbook is the result of input from a wide variety of sources. I am sure there will be discrepancies noted, and I assume full responsibility for all statements in this Handbook.

I would welcome any comments or criticisms on the content of this work.

Dr. Frederick L. Dembowski
SUNY at Albany
1400 Washington Avenue Room 344
Albany, NY 12222
July 1982

INTRODUCTION

A recent headline in a New York newspaper stated "School Districts Flunk Investment 101!" The basis of the article was a study conducted by a research team commissioned by the New York Legislature to investigate how well school districts were investing their surplus funds. The impetus of the study was a feeling on the part of the legislature that school districts were not taking full advantage of the revenue potential of sound cash management. Another study by the author indicated that well over $1 billion were earned on school district investments in the United States in the 1980-81 school year. With these large amounts of revenue at stake, it is no wonder that cash management and the ancillary field of school/banking relations have become recognized as increasingly important functions in school business operations.

The purposes of this publication are two fold: to discuss the major aspects of a school district cash management and banking program; and to demonstrate how an effective cash management system may be established or improved upon in school districts. Each aspect of cash management will be discussed and further illustrated by examples.

A Handbook for School District Financial Management

SECTION I

AN OVERVIEW OF SCHOOL DISTRICT FINANCIAL MANAGEMENT OPERATIONS

CASH management - the process of managing monies in order to ensure maximum cash availability and maximum yield on investments of idle cash - represents an increasingly important component of financial management in a school district. Cash management is concerned with what happens between the time cash is received as revenue and when it is expended. More specifically, cash management is concerned with the conversion of accounts receivable to cash receipts, accounts payable to cash disbursements, the rate at which cash disbursements clear the bank and what is done with cash in the meantime.

There are a number of financial and nonfinancial goals of an effective cash management program in a school district. The primary financial goals of cash management are to maximize availability and yield.

The availability goal is to maximize the amount of cash available to meet daily needs and to increase cash available for investment. The yield goal is to earn the maximum return on cash invested.

These goals conflict with each other to the extent that cash invested may not be readily available to meet current obligations. Since bills must be paid, the yield goal is necessarily secondary. However, the timing of cash inflows and outflows may be manipulated to favorably affect yield.

Additional financial goals include the minimization of the monetary and manpower costs of the cash management process and the minimization of borrowing unless such borrowing is advantageous to a district, such as through an arbitrage situation.

While not as lucrative, the nonfinancial goals of cash management are equally as important to a school district. The most important nonfinancial goals include promoting favorable business relations with vendors and banks; ensuring the orderly conduct of the financial aspects of a district's operations; and building the trust and goodwill of the taxpaying community.

There are eight interrelated components in an effective school district cash management program. When properly coordinated, these elements assure the attainment of a school district's financial and nonfinancial cash management goals. The first component of an effective school district cash management program is an appropriate administrative framework. Such a framework is necessary to attain the financial goals of maximum availability and maximum yield. The next four elements are concerned with cash availability.

They are: cash budgeting; cash information and control systems; cash collection, deposit and disbursement procedures; and borrowing. When successfully managed, these elements promote maximum availability of cash for a district's financial operations. The final three elements of a school district's cash management program are concerned with the goal of maximizing potential yield. These are: investment securities; investment strategies; and school-banking relations. When all eight elements of an effective cash management program are established and skillfully utilized, a school district can realize the full potential of an efficient, successful cash management program.

The Administrative Framework of Cash Management

The administrative framework describes the policy as well as the legal and procedural requirements for carrying out an effective cash management program on a day-to-day basis. In order to contribute to the achievement of cash management goals, a school district, like any local government unit, must have the following:

* a set of Federal, state and local laws that affect the operation of a cash management program;

* a written district policy approved by the Board governing the conduct of the cash management program;

* a cash investment "pool" or consolidation account consisting of the cash balances of different funds and accounts; and

* an on-going evaluation process that periodically reviews progress throughout the fiscal year and provides appropriate historical performance data.

<u>Legal Requirements</u> - Every state has restrictions on the cash management activities of local school districts. These state laws generally restrict cash management in three ways: they stipulate the dates and procedures to be followed in collecting taxes and fees; they restrict the kinds of securities and obligations a school district may utilize for investments and borrowings; and many states limit the types of financial institutions with which local districts may do business. For example, some states prohibit the use of mutual savings banks and out of state banks. A general listing of these statutory restrictions is not feasible here because all the states are different. Section III of this publication has a state by state summary and analysis of many of these differences.

Written District Policy - Within the framework of these legal requirements, a school district should establish a written statement which defines policies relative to cash management. A typical policy adopted by a Board of Education might cover the following items:

1) the delegation of authority for the cash management activities to one district official;

2) a listing of the types of investment instruments in which the district may invest;

3) the criteria for selecting the district's depository bank(s);

4) the specifications about the frequency and types of financial reports that must be submitted to the board; and

5) local district limitations on cash management.

In writing a policy statement, specifying policies, constraints and limitations is necessary. However, the specification of procedures should be avoided and left to the discretion to administrative personnel. An example of a school board policy is presented as Exhibit I.

Cash Investment Pooling - The "pooling" of cash resources consists of consolidating the cash accounts of separate funds into one or a few bank accounts for investment purposes. Often these accounts are called "clearing", "zero-based", or "consolidation" accounts. Pooling need not be restricted to accounts within one district. Where permitted by law, school districts should investigate the establishment of pooling arrangements with other governmental units such as neighboring school districts, nearby city and municipal governments and county governments. Some states have established statewide pooling arrangements. Others have established trust funds for investment purposes.

Where permitted, pooling offers school districts many advantages: it permits larger investments which often yield higher rates of return; it tends to smoothen out fluctuations in cash flow; it simplifies the investment process; and it reduces paperwork.

Under a typical pooling operation, accounting records are kept for the pooled account that attributes cash and investments to each fund and account that contributes to the pooling arrangement. Interest earnings are apportioned accordingly.

EXHIBIT I

SAMPLE SCHOOL BOARD POLICY STATEMENT

1. <u>Purpose and Safeguards</u>:

   The Investment program of the school district is authorized by the Board of Education. It is viewed as a critical ingredient of sound fiscal management, the purpose of which is to secure a maximum yield of interest revenues to supplement other school district revenues for the support of the educational program of the school system.

   The district's investment program will be administered in such a way as to assure:

   a. The continual process of temporary investing of all fund balances and monies available to the district for investment purposes;

   b. The maintenance (revised following each cash transaction) of a yearly cash flow chart that will provide data to assist proper planning and decision making regarding amount, duration, and type of investments for the school district;

   c. The utilization of an open competition system of bids and/or quotes to obtain maximum yield possible on all investments from both in-direct and out-of-district financial institutions;

   d. That all vendors using school district funds provide a statement to the district of their collateral in the form of a list of the securities pledged at market value; and

   e. That all school district investments will be in compliance with Sections 1723-a and 2131 of the Education Law.

2. <u>Delegation of Authority</u>

   The school district authorizes its school business administrator and/or the supervisor of accounting to manage all activities associated with its investment program in such manner as to accomplsh all the objectives and the intents of this policy. These responsibilities will also include annual review and assessment of district's investment program and filing a report and his/her recommendations annually with the Board of Education. The school business administrator is further authorized to execute in the name of the board of education any and all documents relating to the investment program in a timely manner as well as to utilize reputable consultants regarding investment decisions when necessary. A monthly progress report of investments will be given to the board.

Evaluation Processes - Evaluation of cash management performance completes the administrative cycle. It tells interested parties how successful a program has been and establishes a basis for developing objectives for future years' cash management programs. Many studies have reported the rate of return on investments as an evaluative indicator of cash management performance in school districts. For example, McCanless reported an average rate of return on investments of 0.3 percent of the total district expenditures. Both Carr and Rothrock reported average rates of return of 0.078 percent to 0.079 percent of total district expenditures. Welliver reported a range for the rates of return for school districts in Pennsylvania of from 3.29 percent to 0.1 percent with an average rate of return of 0.5 percent of total district expenditures. These rate of return measures point out the need for increased vigor in school district financial management programs.

However, the cash management operations of school districts are not evaluated correctly if the rate of return measure is the only evaluative technique used because the efficiency of these operations is affected by a number of exogenous and endogenous factors. All of these factors affect the net rate of return on the school district's cash management operation. The exogenous factors include current market conditions and the size and the wealth of a school district. The endogenous factors include the mix of investment instruments used, the cash management techniques used and the level of expertise of a district's business staff.

The current rate of interest for investments has the most immediate impact on the rate of return. Generally, the higher the rate of interest (other things being equal), the higher the rate of return. However, interest rates vary greatly over time according to the type and maturity of investment instrument used. In order to make comparisons of the rates of return to school district cash management programs, the evaluation measures should be adjusted to account for the exogenous portion of this varying interest rate.

The size and wealth of a district also have considerable effects on the rate of return. Several studies (See Dembowski, 1980, for a review of these studies) have disclosed that there are scale effects in the rates of return. Generally, the larger the school district, the larger the cash flows, thus the larger the cash surplus available for investment. This problem is further exacerbated by the fact that bankers pay a premium through higher bids for the use of large amounts of cash for investments. Thus, a banker may bid only 10 percent for a certificate of deposit (CD) for 90 days on $100,000 while he may bid 12 percent for a 90 day CD on $1 million. These scale effects should be eliminated in any evaluation of cash management performance.

Furthermore, studies have shown that a district's wealth also has an effect on cash management results. Wynn states that the wealthier the school district, the greater the possibility for school district investment activity (Wynn, 1973). This is partially due to the facts that the timing and amounts of revenues are determined, to a certain extent, by school district wealth.

School district revenues consist primarily of receipts from two sources: property tax collections and state aid receipts. Property tax receipts are based on a school district's property wealth. Studies have shown a direct correlation between school district wealth and expenditures for education. Because more dollars are involved, it logically follows that the higher a school district's expenditures, the greater the potential for surplus cash balances to be available for investment purposes.

However, the effect of wealth on state aid receipts is more direct. Most state aid allocation formulas, because of the desire to equalize educational expenditure disparities caused by differences in wealth, result in poorer school districts receiving a greater proportion of their total expenditures through state aid. Thus, the poorer the district, the more cash received in state aid. The cash management problem that arises from this phenomenon is that receipts from property taxes usually accrue to the school districts only once a year, while state aid receipts are spread throughout the fiscal year.

For example, in New York State, school districts receive a large majority of their property tax receipts (all except for late tax payments) in October, while 75 percent of the state aid is not allocated to the districts until the months of March, April and May in 25 percent installments. With the fiscal year beginning July 1, the property wealth poor school district receives relatively little cash "up front" through the property tax receipts, with the bulk of receipts flowing to the district in the latter months of the fiscal year. This has two implications for a poor district. First, a district that is poorer in property wealth is forced to borrow to a greater extent than a property rich district with the resultant loss of the interest paid on the borrowed funds. Second, the district that is poorer in terms of property wealth has fewer opportunities to invest funds because there are fewer, if any, periods of surplus cash.

Unfortunately, when a business manager's cash management performance in a property wealth poor district is evaluated, the typical measure is the rate of return, expressed as a ratio of the net interest earnings from cash management to the total expenditure of the district. In such districts, the rate of return is much lower than in a rich district because of the difference in timing of cash flow.

An Overview

The endogenous factors listed above also have an effect on the cash management program of a school district. Obviously, the use of different types of investment instruments will affect the rate of return because the interest rate of each instrument or security varies with the degree of risk inherent in the instrument. For example, a future in commodities is much riskier than an investment in U.S. Treasury Bills because it is less likely that the U.S. Government will default on its loans. However, generalities about interest rates are difficult because the term structure of interest rates varies greatly over time for a wide variety of reasons, with risk being one.

Easier to defend is the effect of the training of the business manager in cash management techniques on the rate of return on investments. Most studies agree that the higher the level of training of the cash manager (although not necessarily in cash management), the higher the rate of return on cash management. (See Dembowski, 1978). Finally, the rate of return on cash management will differ depending on the sophistication of the cash management techniques used. While the development of a cash flow schedule for cash planning purposes will enable a business manager to develop a set of investments for a district, the use of optimization techniques, such as an integer programming formulation to optimize the set of investments and borrowings, will most likely result in higher net interest earnings.

There are a number of evaluative techniques that could be used that would eliminate the effects of the exogenous variables from the evaluation, focusing attention on those management practices which the cash manager has control over and can change to a school district's benefit. One such technique is the use of Net Present Value Analysis. The discussion of this technique is beyond the scope of this Handbook. For further discussion of this topic, see Dembowski (1980).

The final topic in the discussion of the administrative component of cash management is the establishment of a standard of evaluation for a school district's cash management performance. As seen in the previous section, there are a number of considerations that must be taken into account when evaluating a cash management program. The rate of return measure typically used to judge cash management performance is not a valid measure for a number of reasons. However, it is very simple to calculate, and will be used for a long while to come. Therefore, its use must be discussed. Because the conditions for cash management programs vary according to state laws and other factors, the establishment of a "good" rate of return is difficult to calculate. Many studies of cash management performance agree that a rate of return of 1.5 percent of a district's total expenditures should be attainable by all school districts, regardless of size, wealth and the other intervening factors. If all school districts in the United States could attain a rate of return of 1.5 percent, approximately $2.5 billion could be earned annually through sound school district cash management programs.

Cash Budgeting

Cash budgeting involves the estimation of receipts and disbursements to determine cash requirements and to develop a cash management strategy. Cash budgeting answers questions such as these:

When are cash receipts expected?

How long will cash be available?

Is borrowing required?

Are there opportunities for investment?

Cash budgeting is different than the "traditional" revenue and expenditure budgeting process because it is primarily concerned with the timing of receipts and disbursements of a school district. The "regular" budgeting process is concerned with the timing and sources of revenues, and the determination of anticipated expenditures. This budgeting process usually precedes the cash budgeting process. Furthermore, while the revenue and expenditure budgeting process culminates with a budget document, cash budgeting is a continual process with periodic updates.

Cash budgeting is important to an effective cash management program because detailed knowledge of the timing and amounts of cash receipts and disbursements allows the manager to take an informed approach to designing an investment and borrowing strategy. Cash budgeting also is important in gathering necessary information to develop the financial position statement needed to borrow cash, especially borrowings based upon future assets such as Revenue Anticupation Notes (RANs) and Tax Anticipation Notes (TANs).

An important tool in cash budgeting is the cash flow schedule. A cash flow schedule may be as simple as a table which lists total expected receipts, disbursements and net balances by month (as in Exhibit II) or as detailed as a listing of receipts and disbursements by fund and source on a weekly or even daily basis (as in Exhibit III).

In constructing a cash flow schedule, two critical parameters must be established. First, a time horizon must be selected. A school district should always develop an annual cash flow schedule for its fiscal year. By including all major receipts and disbursements for the entire year, this annual schedule will indicate per-

An Overview

EXHIBIT II

THE CASH FLOW PATTERN OF THE SAMPLE DISTRICT

Period	1	2	3	4	5	6	7	8	9	10	11	12	13
Month	Jan. 1	Feb. 1	Mar. 1	Apr. 1	May 1	June 1	July 1	Aug. 1	Sept. 1	Oct. 1	Nov. 1	Dec. 1	Dec. 31
Inflow	400	250	400	150	100	50	50	50	150	400	400	50	0
Outflow	200	200	200	200	200	400	100	100	200	200	200	300	0
Netflow	+200	+50	+200	+200	-100	-350	-50	-50	-50	+200	+200	-250	0

Revenues are received by the district on the first day of the month.

Expenditures occur on the first day of the month.

Beginning cash balance of the district on the first day of the year is $50,000.

EXHIBIT III

SAMPLE CASH FLOW CHART

FOR THE PERIOD - JULY 1 to OCTOBER 1

Date	Explanation	Estimated Expenditures	Estimated Revenues	Running Balance
July 1	Opening cash balance (not fund balance)	$	$	$247,000
14	Payroll	37,000		210,000
28	Payroll	40,000		170,000
31	Bills	30,000		140,000
Aug 1	Debt, Principal & Interest	63,000		77,000
11	Payroll	37,000		40,000
15	Bills	40,000		0
25	Tax Anticipation Note		400,000	400,000
25	Payroll	40,000		360,000
31	Bills	50,000		310,000
Sept 1	Debt, Principal & Interest	63,000		247,000
1	Payroll	200,000		47,000
10	Bills	40,000		7,000
15	State Aid		350,000	357,000
15	Payroll	200,000		157,000
20	Bills	60,000		97,000
29	Property Tax		1,400,000	1,497,000
29	Pay TAN	400,000		1,097,000

iods of major borrowing and investment requirements. Once an annual schedule has been developed, cash flow schedules for smaller periods (such as bi-annual, monthly, bi-weekly or weekly) may be developed. In general, the smaller the time horizon, the more time-consuming and costly the cash budgeting process becomes. Thus, the cash manager must weigh the costs and benefits to the district of a detailed cash budgeting process.

The second decision essential to cash budgeting is the level of specification involved in the cash flow schedule. The cash manager must decide upon a level of aggregation in specifying the cash receipts and disbursements and the time interval for reporting. For example, Exhibit II represents a cash flow schedule in which a cash manager has made two decisions. First, it is an annual cash flow schedule representing a fiscal year, with data reported in monthly intervals. Second, only total monthly receipts and disbursements are reported with no disaggregation of the data. In contrast, Exhibit III is a three-month cash flow chart with receipts and disbursements disaggregated into major categories reported on the day of anticipated receipt or disbursement. This more detailed cash flow schedule will enable a cash manager to make more precise estimates of the cash needs of a district.

In order to develop a cash flow schedule, the timing and amounts of cash receipts and disbursements must be anticipated. Historical cash flow information is invaluable for this purpose, and it is recommended that records of the dates and amounts of major receipts and disbursements of the district be kept in memorandum accounts. It is also possible to review previous years' cash accounts for this purpose. School districts receive most of their revenues through property taxes and state aid payments. Both types of payments accrue to the district in large lump sums received periodically throughout the fiscal year. The property taxes, which account for 40 to 60 percent of an average district's revenues, are usually received by the district once or twice a year. These annual or semi-annual payment periods (usually lasting a week or two) result in substantial amounts of cash flowing into a school district's coffers at specific times of the year.

State aid payments are usually the second largest source of school district revenue. While the timing and amounts of state aid payments to school districts vary from state to state, these payments are also quite large. Together, property tax and state aid receipts comprise the majority of school district revenues, typically accounting for 70 to 85 percent of the total income to a district. Fortunately, both the timing and amounts of these receipts are known in advance with a high degree of certainty. This certainty enables a cash manager to accurately project the receipt of these funds and aids in the development of a cash flow schedule.

Besides being able to anticipate revenues with a high degree of certainty, expenditures may also be anticipated. School district expenditures consist primarily of salary and fringe benefit expenses. The typical school district budget allots approximately 80 percent of all expenditures for this purpose. Once the number of employees is determined, and the salary schedule is negotiated, these expenditures may be anticipated with a high degree of certainty. Except for the summer months, the expenditure pattern of most school districts is quite stable. Other major expenses, such as debt service payments and utility bills may also be anticipated through a review of the previous year's expenditure patterns. June is usually the highest expenditure month because of social security and tax payments to the Federal Government as well as end of the year payments to teachers and vendors.

Exhibit IV presents a simplified revenue and expenditure pattern for the hypothetical school district cash flow projection presented in Exhibit II. October and January revenues are large because of property tax receipts while the November and March receipts reflect state aid payments. Expenditures are stable at $200,000 for most months, with a peak in June and low expenses in the summer months. Because of differences in the timing and amounts of revenues and expenditures, the school district experiences periods of surplus revenues over expenditures, denoted by "S". January through March is a period of surplus cash. From April through October, however, the school district's expenditures exceed it's revenues. These periods of cash deficits are denoted as "D". The primary task of the cash manager in this hypothetical school district is to determine what borrowing and investing decisions should be made. If investments are made, three questions must be answered:

When should investments be made?

What amounts should be invested?

How long should the cash be invested?

If it is necessary to borrow, the same questions concerning timing, amount and maturity need to be answered.

This financial planning task is usually approached in the following manner. The net cash flow is determined by subtracting monthly expenditures from monthly revenues. A positive (negative) net cash flow indicates a cash surplus (deficit). Exhibit II presents the monthly cash flows in tabular form. The month of January

An Overview 15

EXHIBIT IV

THE CASH BUDGET AND CASH FLOW PATTERN OF THE SAMPLE DISTRICT

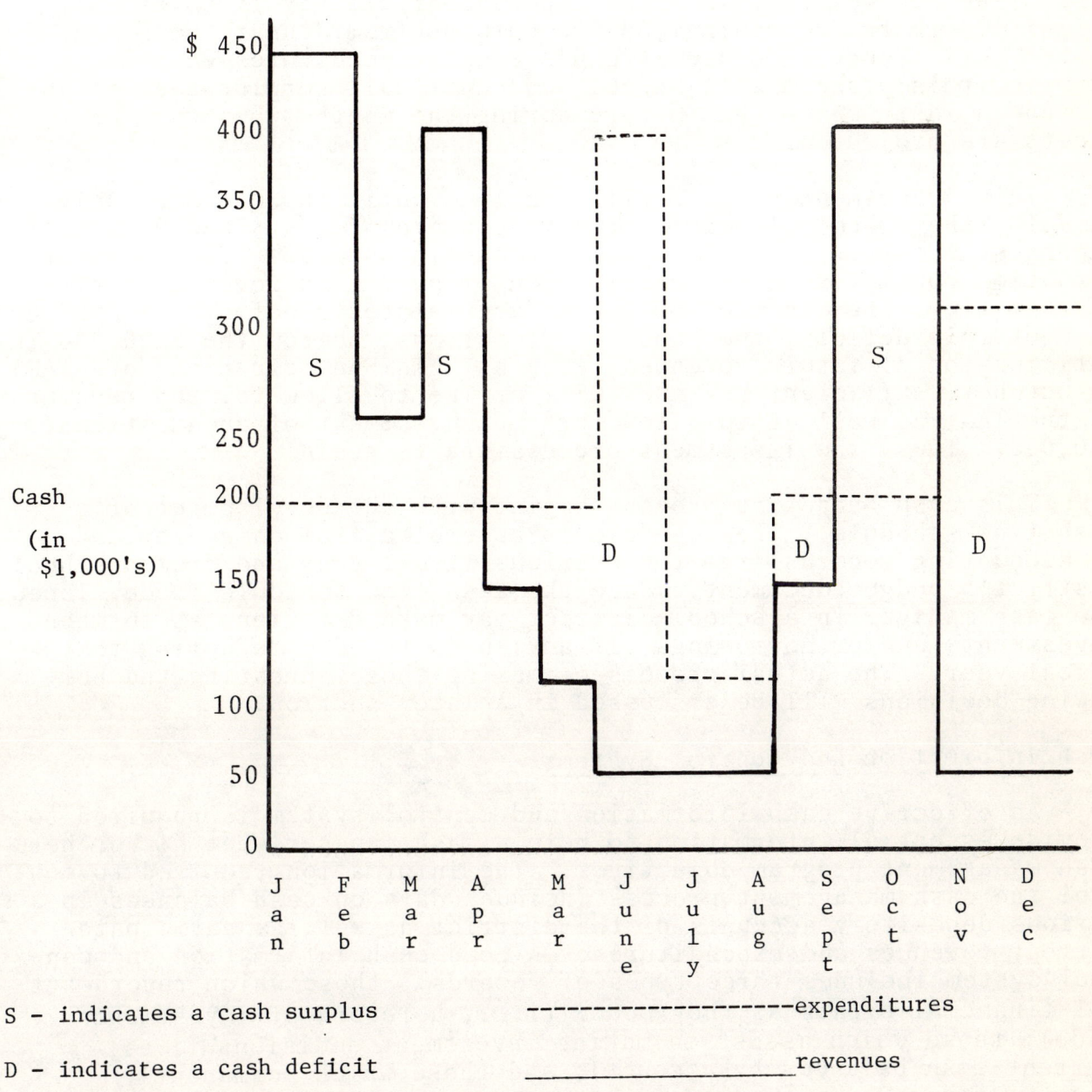

S - indicates a cash surplus   ---------------------expenditures

D - indicates a cash deficit   _____revenues

has a $200,000 cash surplus. This cash should be invested in interest bearing securities (such as Certificates of Deposit or Repurchase Agreements). Since the month of April has a cash deficit of $50,000, an investment of $50,000 should be made from January to April. Another $100,000 could be invested from January to May to cover that deficit, with the remaining $50,000 surplus from January being invested until June. Because revenues equal expenditures in this example, this process will be followed until all surplus cash is invested in instruments that mature during the months when cash deficits are projected.

This investment process will continue until the month of July. In July, the school district (in this example) needs $50,000 to meet expenses. However, all available revenue is used up. This deficit situation continues until October when property tax revenues arrive. By that time, the district will have accumulated a deficit of $150,000. To meet this deficit, the school district must borrow the $150,000 in anticipation of future revenues (such as a Tax Anticipation Note-TAN). In October, sufficient revenues will arrive to allow for the repayment of the TAN, as well as to allow for the investment of an additional $50,000. Thus, the investment process starts again.

This cash budgeting process begins with the development of a cash flow schedule. The schedule is assembled from data provided by accounting records from the previous fiscal year and from a school district's budget document. Once the cash flow schedule is developed, the cash manager in a school district may make decisions as to when investments and/or borrowings (if any) need to be made during that fiscal year. The actual process of making these investing and borrowing decisions will be discussed in a later section.

Cash Information and Control Systems

An effective cash information and control system is required to provide essential information to help a cash manager meet his or her cash management program objectives. The information required to control the cash management process includes data on cash balances in various depository accounts of the district as well as anticipated current revenues and expenditures. A good cash information and control system includes three types of records: those which record actual financial events as they occur (i.e., a record of investments made); those which assist in making investment decisions (i.e., current cash balances by account); and those which permanently account for cash by fund.

A cash information and control system typically has two major components: a formal system and an informal system. The formal system consists of accounting processes that systematically record appropriate data. A "Cash Accounting System" should keep track of daily receipts and disbursements, provide cash balances by fund and account and record daily average cash balances. A "Cash Budget Reporting System" should be implemented to provide a "budget vs. actual" report of receipts and disbursements. This system provides information to update a cash flow schedule and to evaluate a cash manager's forecasting abilities.

An "Investment Status and Earnings System" is useful in providing a summary performance record of cash management activities. Key information on investment transactions that should be recorded are the purchase (date, amount and rate), the sale (date and amount), the maturity and the interest. A similar record system, if needed, is the "Earned Interest Apportionment System" which is required if the interest must be redistributed to the accounts and funds which contributed cash to the principal of the investment.

A "Reconciliation System" is required to provide data to undertake a monthly reconciliation between the balance in accounting records and the actual cash balances in bank accounts and other assets of the school district. The reconciliation usually follows this basic format to determine Ending Cash Balance:

Cash in Treasury
plus Investment Principal
plus Cash in Banks
minus Outstanding Checks
minus Deposits Not Yet Recorded

equals Ending Cash Balance

Finally, a "Performance Reporting System" should be designed to provide information required to assess how well a district's cash management system is performing in relation to attaining the four objectives of availability, yield, dollars earned and efficiency of operation. Performance reporting warrants special attention to procedure reports for those instances when an evaluation is required (when estimating interest received during the budgeting process).

A well administered cash information and control system also has an important informal system. This informal system consists of good contact with responsible officers in the various departments of a school district to provide information on anticipated cash flow needs which the cash manager may be unaware of. Information concerning current market conditions, vendor relations and so on are also of importance.

Cash Collection, Deposit and Disbursement Procedures

Cash collection, deposit and disbursement procedures are possibly the most important factors in determining the maximum availability of funds to meet cash needs and maximize the return on investment of funds. The development of procedures to bring revenue dollars into district accounts as soon as possible and to keep those dollars there as long as possible can mean a significant increase in investment dollars earned. To ensure that these processes will contribute to achieving cash management goals, a school district should have:

1) revenue collection policies and procedures for each major source of revenue;

2) special deposit procedures to handle major revenue processing problems such as tax collections;

3) established deposit procedures for each type of revenue and collection location; and

4) disbursement policies and procedures for each category of expenditure and vendor.

Collections can be greatly accelerated if a school district develops procedures designed to encourage the speedy payment of property taxes. Some suggested procedures are as follows:

Increase the frequency of property tax collections. This will allow the receipt of cash to more closely align with expected disbursements, and will smoothen out the cyclical cash flow patterns permitting larger and longer investments.

* Raise the penalties for delinquent payments to discourage the practice of deferring payment and holding money for more personally productive purposes.

* Offer discounts to encourage prepayments. This is only advantageous if the discounts do not cost more than the expected earnings on the cash made available.

* Provide preaddressed and/or prepaid postage return envelopes to encourage rapid payment.

* Use banking services including lockboxes, bank collections and so on.

The receipt of many other forms of tax revenues received by a school district can be accelerated by working closely with Federal, state and local governmental agencies responsible for distributing the cash to school districts. For example, lobbying with other school districts at the state level might be effective in producing earlier payment of state aid monies. It is also important to ensure that the required forms and claims are submitted complete and in a timely manner so that revenues are received when expected.

Deposit procedures affect the rate at which money already on its way to a school district is deposited into a bank account. One example in New York State is that districts in the far Western portion of the state send a courier to the state capital (250 miles away) to collect state aid checks instead of having them mailed. While this practice sounds trivial, it can generate additional funds. For example, if a $2 million state aid check were picked up, driven back and deposited on the same day it was issued into a Repurchase Agreement for three days (the normal time for delivery to the school district by mail) at 15 percent interest, the district could earn $2,465.70 minus the cost of the trip! There are a number of other special arrangements that can be made to speed up deposits.

Many banks accept direct deposits of mailed property tax payments under a lock box system. A lock box arrangement allows cash to be immediately deposited into a district's accounts, thereby removing a step in the deposit process and allowing payments to become immediately available for use upon receipt. Depositing funds in branch offices of a depository bank will also speed up the collection and deposit process.

Another widely used method of speeding up revenues into district coffers is through the use of wire transfers. Money transfer requests can be received from a number of sources. Because of risks associated with the processing of wires, items must be tightly controlled. All requests are first routed to a pre-processing center. This center is responsible for preparing all payments for transmission and forwarding to the processing area. The steps required to prepare the transfer include:

1) checking all requests for authenticity;

2) identifying credit and debit parties;

3) deciding on the method of payment;

4) checking for availability of sufficient funds; and

5) indexing and obtaining authorized approval.

The payments processing area is responsible for the actual transfer of funds. Each transfer is formatted on an Automated Funds Transfer System (AFTS) and verified by a second series of checks. Member banks of the Federal Reserve System are able to utilize their wire transfer system, the Federal Interface System (FIS), to send a Federal Funds Transfer. Transfers are transmitted through FIS to the money transfer system of the bank involved. The deadline for all Federal Fund Transfers is 4:30 P.M., thus the arrangements for the wire transfer must be made earlier in the day with the sending bank. Most banks also have time deadlines.

There are also a number of methods which may be used by school districts to manage the disbursement process in a manner favorable to the district's cash management program. From the cash management standpoint, disbursements should be timed so that they remove cash from the district's accounts at the last possible moment. However, the incentive must be tempered by the need to pay bills in a timely fashion. Unhappy vendors may raise prices, perform poorly or require excessive administrative time in responding to complaints.

One effective system is to schedule specific payroll and vendor payment days each month. Over time, this practice will result in routine scheduled disbursements which are "tailor-made" for cash management practices. An accounts payable system which allows payables to "age" before payment can improve disbursement control. As invoices are received, they should be briefly analyzed and a payment date affixed. They can then be paid on the payment date instead of immediately. Some factors that affect the payment date are: discounts available, past history of a vendor requiring immediate payment and the method of payment (i.e., mail payment, hand delivery and so on).

Discounts may result in significant savings. For example, a discount of 1 percent for payment in 10 days as opposed to no discount when the full bill is due in 30 days, is equivalent to an interest rate of 18 percent annually.

Warrants can be used to improve cash availability in certain instances. A warrant is a promise to pay a sum of money at some future date upon presentation to the issuer. Under a warrant system, funds need not be available until the date the warrant is presented to the issuer for payment. One disadvantage is that banks usually charge higher handling charges for warrants than checks. Vendor relations is also an important consideration in changing disbursement procedures. Good communication and a history of good relationships with vendors can carry a school district over a rough financial period. For example, instead of borrowing cash for a very short period of anticipated deficit, it might be to the district's

An Overview

advantage to delay payment to a vendor for the deficit period.

A final issue of importance in discussing disbursements is the direct deposit of payrolls. In direct payroll deposit, the district enjoys favorable employee relations because it is easier for the employees to access their money. Banks like direct payroll deposit because it brings them new customers and increases their cash balances. However, from a cash management standpoint, direct deposit of payroll is unfavorable to the school district because it speeds up the flow of cash from district accounts significantly, thus shortening the time available to the district for investing the cash.

What difference would these few days mean in cash management terms? As an example, suppose a school district paid its employees on Friday afternoons every two weeks and that each payroll amounts to $200,000. Under a direct payroll deposit system all this cash would leave the district's accounts on Friday afternoon. However, an analysis of the school district's bank statements of the payroll account for the prior fiscal year would have revealed the cash flow pattern shown in Exhibit V. On the Friday paydays, only 25.5 percent of the paychecks were cashed and cleared the bank. The remaining 74.5 percent of the payroll stayed in the checking account over the weekend. On Monday night, an additional 31 percent of the payroll checks cleared the bank and so on. If a school district had a policy to leave only 30 percent of its payroll in its checking account to cover Friday's checks, it could have placed the remaining $149,000 in a three-day Repurchase Agreement with the bank. These instruments typically earn 15 percent annually. In this case, a school district, using this procedure, could have earned an additional $186.15 every two weeks or more than $4,000 during a fiscal year. Thus, a direct payroll deposit system needs to be considered very carefully before being established.

Borrowing

There are times when a school district may require cash in excess of anticipated revenues. At such times, the district may borrow cash through a variety of means. There are two classes of borrowing: long-term and short-term. Long-term borrowing provides a school district with a large sum of money, usually for a specific purpose, such as the construction of a building, which is paid off over a specified period of years. Long-term borrowing, and the ancillary topic of capital debt management, are beyond the scope of this publication. Short-term borrowing allows a district to meet current obligations for a period prior to the receipt of anticipated cash. Both types of borrowing are an integral part of a sound cash management system.

EXHIBIT V

PAYROLL DISBURSEMENT PATTERN

DAY	CHECKS CASHED	PERCENT CASHED
Friday	$ 51,000	25.5
Monday	62,000	31.0
Tuesday	33,000	16.5
Wednesday	8,000	4.0
Thursday	5,000	2.5
Friday	5,000	2.5
Monday	20,000	10.0
Tuesday	9,000	4.5
Wednesday	5,000	2.5
Thursday	2,000	1.0
Total	$200,000	100%

The purpose of short-term borrowing is to provide sufficient cash for a school district to meet its current obligations during an interim period of cash deficit. The cash is usually borrowed in anticipation of revenues expected in the near future. Short-term borrowing is avoided by many school districts, possibly because of the severe restrictions placed on school districts by statutory law. However, short-term borrowing should be considered an important tool in an effective cash management program and could offer opportunities for net interest earnings for a school district.

There are generally five types of obligations available to school districts for short-term borrowing:

1) Revenue Anticipation Notes (RAN) - used for general purposes in anticipation of collected revenues other than property taxes (state aid, for example);

2) Tax Anticipation Notes (TAN) - used for general purposes in anticipation of taxes or assessments levied or to be levied;

3) Bond Anticipation Notes (BAN) - may be issued whenever bonds have been authorized. The proceeds may be used only for the same object or purpose for which the bond may be expended;

4) Budget Notes - used to provide revenues during the fiscal year for any unforeseeable public emergency. These notes are usually paid off with taxes collected in the following fiscal year; and

5) Capital Notes - used to finance all or part of the cost of any object or purpose for which serial or sinking fund bonds may be issued. Capital Notes are usually issued for a two-year period.

The use of these short-term borrowing instruments is usually restricted by statutory law. Most states have limitations on the payback period, amount and reinvestment opportunities of borrowed funds. The payback periods vary widely from state to state with the most common periods being either by the end of the fiscal year in which funds were borrowed or six months. However, many states authorize longer payback periods for specific short-term obligations. In Texas, for example, Budget Notes and Contract Obligation Notes have a payback period of 25 years.

Many states also limit the amount which may be borrowed on a short-term basis. Again these restrictions vary from state to state and according to the particular obligation used. The norm for general short-term borrowing through TANs and RANs is that 75 to

80 percent of the anticipated revenue can be borrowed through these notes. Some states allow 100 percent of the anticipated revenues to be borrowed, while others allow only 25 percent.

Finally, the majority of states in the United States allow borrowed monies to be reinvested until needed for current obligations. This practice offers school districts the opportunity to earn net interest over the cost of the borrowed cash through investment. This opportunity is due to the fact that the interest rates available to school districts on borrowed cash is usually substantially less than the rates available through investments. This differential in interest rates exists because cash loaned to school districts is tax exempt, and lending institutions, such as banks, can offer lower interest rates on loans to school districts because of this tax savings. The "point spread" or difference between the borrowing and investing rate offers school districts the opportunity to "make" money by borrowing and then investing a portion of the proceeds. This practice is commonly referred to as "arbitrage".

As an example of arbitrage, consider the following situation: The school district cash flow which is displayed in Exhibit II will experience an anticipated cash deficit of $150,000 during the months of July, August and September. There will be sufficient revenues flowing into the school district in October ($200,000) to pay back a TAN to cover this deficit. The school district is able to borrow the needed $150,000 through its local bank for 10 percent annual interest. The current rate of interest on investments is 15 percent annual interest.

The school district has a number of options. The first is to borrow the $150,000 on July 1 and pay it back on October 1 when it will have sufficient revenues to do so. In this case, the school district would use $50,000 to cover the deficit in July, invest $50,000 until August 1 to cover that deficit and invest $50,000 for two months, until September 1, to cover the September deficit. It would pay back the TAN on October 1. Thus, the school district would earn $1,875 in interest on its investments, but pay the bank $3,748.50 on the borrowed cash, a net loss to the district of $1,873.50.

However, the school district has several other options. Suppose that the cash manager of the school district read the arbitrage regulations of the state carefully and discovered that the deficit cash can be legally borrowed at the beginning of the fiscal year in which the anticipated deficit will occur, and does not have to be paid back until the end of the fiscal year. Further, the law states that a school district may legally borrow one months expenditure in addition to the anticipated deficit. (This hypothetical law is modeled after the arbitrage regulations that existed in New York State in 1981!).

Following this law, the school district cash manager determined that there was a deficit of $150,000 and that the average expenditure for most months was $200,000. He then determined that he could borrow $350,000 at the beginning of the fiscal year on January 1 at a rate of 10 percent, invest $200,000 until December 31 because it was not needed to cover a deficit but was being used only as a reserve. He then invested $50,000 on January 1 until July 1 to cover the July deficit; invested $50,000 until August 1 to cover that month's deficit; and invested the remaining $50,000 on January 1 until September 1 to cover that month's investment. While strictly following the limits of the law in that state, the school district would earn a total of $48,750 on investments (don't forget the additional $150,000 in October), and pay $35,000 in December on the borrowed cash, for a net interest earning for the school district of $13,750!

Most states have a clearly specified arbitrage policy but the process has been discouraged by the Internal Revenue Service (IRS). A school district obviously enjoys the process because it affords an opportunity to earn additional interest revenues. Taxpayers enjoy lowered local levies. Banks often favor the process because they gain in a number of ways: the interest paid on these investments is tax deductible as a cost of doing business; the interest earned on the note borrowed by the school district is tax-exempt, yielding a much higher effective yield to the bank than the specified 10 percent annual rate; and, the note may be used by the bank as collateral for other investments of the school districts in the area. However, the conditions under which banks may favor the arbitrage process are dependent upon current market conditions and the balance of the bank's portfolio between taxable and non-taxable securities. The only "loser" in this process is the Federal Government and the IRS because tax revenues are reduced due to the tax exemptions and deductions of the banks. Because of IRS admonishments and court opinions, most states have statutory provisions or comptroller opinions limiting this arbitrage process.

A school district may borrow to cover short-term deficits either through its local market or through the major money markets, such as New York, Chicago or San Francisco. In borrowing through its local market, a school district obtains a legal opinion from a local legal firm and markets its borrowing securities through a local bank. Borrowing through the major money markets differs in that securing a legal opinion through a recognized legal firm is very important. Legal firms which are recognized as experts in bonding are listed in the Bond Buyers Directory, also known as the "Red Book". A recognized legal opinion on a bond or note will facilitate the competitive sale of municipal securities, often resulting in a more favorable rate on the bond.

An important marketing tool for bond sales is an Official Statement which provides full disclosure of operations and pertinent information. The official statement makes marketing securities to the public much easier. Once written, a yearly update of the official statement is a simple and inexpensive process.

Banks buy these securities at a risk position. This means that the rate quoted on a security is what the bank feels that it can "live with" and market at a profit. The profit is the spread between the rate the municipality will pay and the rate of return a buyer is willing to accept when purchasing these tax-exempt securities. This risk position of a bank is another reason to use an official statement. Early notification to a bank that a school district is going to need to borrow in the near future allows bank personnel who market the securities to promote an issue and establish a pre-sale list of buyers. The more successful the pre-sale effort, the less risk to the bank and the more aggressive the rate to the school district on its security. Early notice to a bank about the timing of a school district's borrowing needs could result in the avoidance of an unfavorable marketing environment for a district's notes.

For example, suppose a school district in rural Minnesota needed to borrow $1.2 million for six months and decided in advance to offer these notes for sale on April 1. The school district's banker knew from other sources that the City of Minneapolis was also marketing $50 million for a highway project on that day. This would place the school district's notes in an unfavorable marketing position. The bank would not "need" any notes at that time because it was busy trying to market the larger note. Thus, the bank would suggest to the district that it market its notes one week earlier to obtain a more favorable rate.

The municipal security market (school districts are considered a municipality by financial institutions) is an over the counter market versus an auction market such as the New York Stock Exchange. Dealers (banks) actually own the securities they are marketing and must sell them to investors. Traditionally, the largest purchasers of tax-exempt notes and bonds have been other banks and insurance companies. Now, however, the largest purchasers are individuals and surrogate individuals such as money market funds and tax-exempt funds. Other investors include investment banks such as Solomon Brothers, Roosevelt and Cross and Merrill Lynch. The paying agent is usually the successful bidder in a small issue. Payment by a municipality is made to the bank which processes all returned coupons and notes. The paying agent could be someone other than the successful bidding bank, such as the final purchaser of the securities, or a predesignated paying agent.

Districts using local legal opinions to market their notes should understand the effects of these loans on a bank's investment portfolio. Municipal (school district) notes yield a substantially reduced rate of return to a bank because of their tax exempt status. The benefit of this type of security to a bank fluctuates constantly depending upon the current structure of the bank's portfolio. Due to the nature of the market, notes with local legal opinions are more difficult to sell to buyers of tax free securities than securities with legal opinions from recognized bonding firms. This may mean a bank will hold notes in its portfolio. Depending on the size and current portfolio status of a bank, these notes may or may not be desireable. A school business official should contact his banker as soon as his district's borrowing needs are determined. This will allow sufficient time for bank officers to gather the necessary financial information required for credit analysis and approval to loan the needed monies. The information needed by the bank for these purposes includes the district's current budget; its latest audit report; and, for RANs and TANs, a cash flow schedule covering at least the term of the note. Specific information needed for the credit analysis includes the year-end balance of the operating fund; the appropriated fund balance in the current year's budget; revenue projections showing the source to be used for the repayment of the loan; and the cash flow deficit used to jusify the amount to be borrowed according to arbitrage regulations.

"Political Bids" or negotiated sales are an alternative to the formal bidding process. The market rate for the type of paper being offered is a gauge for an actual bid rate that may be substantially higher or lower because of the circumstances at the time of the bid. The school district's business and its depository balances in a bank offer a district leverage in negotiating with a bank on borrowings. Effective use of this leverage can yield substantially reduced rates on borrowings, often lower than those which can be obtained by going through the major money markets or the formal bidding process.

In summary, short-term borrowing should not be shunned or shied away from. It is a valuable cash management tool, and if used wisely, it can result in net interest earnings to a school district. However, there are some very specific procedures that should be followed in marketing notes which have a substantial impact on the rates obtained. A school district's attitude toward borrowing also could have an adverse effect on the cash balances available for investment in its depository accounts with its banks.

Investing

As with borrowing, the investing practices of school districts are strictly regulated by statutory law. The cash manager should have a complete compendium of these laws, legal opinions, comptroller opinions and so on that regulate this process. Only within the scope of what is legally permitted for investing do the other considerations of risk, liquidity and yield apply.

The risk of financial loss should temper all school district investment practices. Even where legally permitted, high risk or speculative investments should be avoided because it is tax payer money that is being risked. To reduce the risk of default or loss, many states require collateral on all school district investments. This collateral requirement varies from state to state. The Federal Deposit Insurance Corporation (FDIC) insures the first $100,000 of all deposits, thus collateral is not needed for investments up to that amount. Despite this insurance, however, some states still require 100 percent collateral on this $100,000. This requirement has the effect of doubly insuring the investment with a school district picking up the tab for the insurance through lower interest rates offered by banks. Banks bid lower on investments that require collateral because the collateral requirement costs the banks cash to maintain the necessary assets instead of using them for other, more lucrative purposes. Some states, such as Kentucky and Mississippi, require more than 100 percent collateral on all investments. These collateral requirements on school district investments is clearly an area which needs legislative attention.

Once the legality and risk of an investment are understood, a cash manager should next consider liquidity and yield. Liquidity is the ability to quickly convert a security to cash without the loss of principal and/or accrued interest. Cash managers should always include some highly liquid securities in a district's portfolio to be assured that all bills will be paid on time in the face of some unanticipated cash deficit.

The yield of investments varies with the type of security used. Competitive bids for comparable investments may indicate different yields available in the securities market. For example, comparable Certificates of Deposit may be purchased at three diffferent banks for three different yields depending upon the banks' need for cash at a given time. Besides the reasons for varying bids from different banks there are a number of factors that will affect the yield of an investment. Generally, the yield is higher when:

* the maturity date is further away;

* the risk is greater;

* the liquidity of the investment is less;

* the denomination of the investment is greater; and

* the investment does not require collateral.

Each security has a defined method for calculating yield. Interest earned is either calculated on a 360 or 365 day basis, causing slight differences in actual interest earnings between bids on two investments with the same maturity. For this reason, in a bid, not only the interest rate, but also the net total interest earnings in dollars should be specified.

Investment Securities

There are many types of securities which school districts may use for investment purposes. The list is growing all the time. Many states limit the types of instruments school districts may use for investments, and the use of each instrument may have unique restrictions. The specific regulations regarding the use of investment securities should be carefully explored and documented. The more common investment instruments used by school districts are these:

Certificates of Deposit (CD) - a time deposit issued against funds deposited in a bank for a specified period of time, usually not less than 14 days nor more than one year. The interest rate is negotiated by the issuing bank and the investor. The minimum amount for a negotiable CD is typically $100,000. There are two types of CDs: a primary CD which is purchased directly from the issuing bank and a secondary CD which is a negotiable CD already issued and traded on the open market. A CD has good marketability in the secondary market, but is limited for amounts less than $1 million. CDs of less than $100,000 are restricted to a maximum rate of 8 percent by Federal Reserve Regulations.

Repurchase Agreements - (or "Repos") - represent an investment in which securities, usually U.S. Treasury Bills, are purchased under an agreement to resell at a later date. A Repo offers maximum security to an investor since the government securities are literally owned by the investor as collateral until repayment at maturity. Maturities are generally short, up to 60 days, but can be written for longer periods. Repos are an ideal, high quality investment for very short periods of time. A reverse Repo can be purchased when an investor is in need of funds. Under this agreement, a bank will purchase government securities under an agreement to sell them back to an investor at a later date for an agreed amount of interest. This can provide investors with significant flexibility in managing their cash position.

U.S. Government Securities - There are two basic types of government securities: U.S. Treasury Bills and Treasury Notes and Bonds. Treasury Bills are government guaranteed securities with maturities of one year or less. Treasury Bills are available with a minimum investment of $10,000 and in $5,000 denominations. The marketability of Treasury Bills in the secondary market is excellent. Since they are sold on a discount basis, an investor pays less than par value for the securities and receives par value at maturity, the difference representing the interest income. Treasury Notes and Bonds are direct obligations of the U.S. Government and are often available in $1,000 denominations with maturities ranging from one to 30 years. Treasury Bonds and Notes also have excellent marketability.

Federal Agency Securities - A number of Federal Government Agencies offer investment securities. Six major obligations in this category are: Banks for Cooperatives (COOPS), Federal Intermediate Credit Banks (FICB), Federal Land Banks (FLB), Federal Home Loan Banks (FHLB), Federal National Mortgage Association (GNMA). Only GNMAs are backed by the full faith and credit of the U.S. Government. The other agencies have the implied backing of the government. Maturities vary depending upon the issuing agency. Marketability is excellent, but not quite as good as for Treasury Bills. In addition to the agencies listed above, there are several lesser known agencies which also offer high quality securities offering good marketability.

State and Municipal Obligations - State and municipal governments offer a wide variety of tax-exempt securities to finance their operations. BANs, TANs and RANs are examples of short-term notes with maturities of less than one year. The security of these notes reflects the credit quality of the issuing entity. Repayment for these notes is made from anticipated revenues.

NOW Accounts (Negotiated Orders of Withdrawal) - NOW accounts offer the liquidity of a depository account with the interest earning capability of a savings account. Most banks currently offer NOW accounts to their customers.

Different securities purchased from different types of institutions may require different procedures, each with unique problems. Most of these are procedural problems and center on the purchase and sale of the security. Some of the most important questions a cash manager should have answered concerning each transaction are these:

Have the terms and the principal, discount and accrued interest amounts been confirmed and recorded?

Is the description of the security in question clear?

Has the method by which the funds are to be delivered been specified?

Has the location where the security will be held for safekeeping been specified?

Has the place where settlement will take place been specified?

What bank accounts will be credited or debited as a result of the transactions?

Answering these questions will help ensure the accurate completion of a transaction without excessive administrative complications and without the risk of failure to complete the transaction.

Investment Strategies

An investment strategy should govern the actions that are taken in the day-to-day cash management program of any district. This strategy should center on the cash management goals of availability and yield discussed earlier. There are three primary inputs of importance in developing an investment strategy. These are:

1) The amount of money available to invest. The cash flow schedule combined with information on current outstanding investments determines the forecast of the amount of cash available for investment.

2) Money market conditions. An analysis of the historical and present money market conditions helps forecast the expected increase or decrease in the yield rates of various types of securities.

3) The mix of securities. The cash control and reporting systems should provide information about the current mix of investments (what investments have been made for what periods of time) representing the investment portfolio at the beginning of the period covered by the investment strategy.

One investment strategy was implicitly assumed in the determination of investment amounts and maturities in the cash budgeting section discussed earlier. In that discussion, the net flow of a sample school district (See Exhibit II) was determined and investments selected based on a manual determination of cash availability and need in later periods. This method is the most basic, and the easiest procedure for investing. Inexperienced cash managers should use it to get their "feet wet". However, it should be noted that because of differences in the term structures of interest rates, substantial amounts of interest earnings could be lost using this method.

For example, suppose the cash manager of the school district represented by Exhibit II were concerned with the period from January to June only, eliminating the necessity to include borrowing in his deliberations. During this six-month period, there are a number of opportunities to invest surplus cash. The important question for the cash manager to answer is: "What investments should be made in order to maximize interest earnings while making sure that all bills are paid?" Unfortunately, this problem is practically insolvable by manual methods because it is too complex. There are a number of computerized techniques that can be used for this purpose (See for example, Dembowski, 1980). However, even if an optimal solution cannot be reached by manual methods, the results obtained by using the basic method discussed above can be improved upon.

In any investment strategy, it is essential that the cash manager keep accurate records of his investments and their maturity dates. One method to do this is called "notation". The cash manager uses the abbreviation "NPtk" for all investments. The "NP" stands for "notes purchased", the "t" is the number of the month in which the investment is purchased, and the "k" is the number of months later the investment matures. Thus, NP13 would represent an investment made in the first period (January) maturing three months later (April). Likewise, NP24 represents an investment made in February and maturing in June.

In the cash budgeting section, a simplified investment pattern was discussed. However, a number of important pieces of information were not revealed in that discussion. This information is primarily concerned with the interest rates available on investments. In the previous section, it was disclosed that interest rates vary according to the maturity of an investment security. Generally, the longer the investment, the higher the interest rate. For this example, suppose the cash manager of a school district called the local banker for the current interest rates on investments. It was determined that an investment in a CD of one to two months duration would earn an annual interest rate of 7 percent, a three to four month investment would earn 9 percent annual interest and an investment of five to six months would earn 11 percent. With this new information, what investments should be made, keeping in mind the goal of maximizing interest earnings?

In this case, the longer the term of the investments, the more interest the school district will earn. In this example, with differing interest rates, the cash manager would most likely make the following investments:

An Overview

1) NP15 = $250,000 resulting in interest of $11,458

2) NP24 = $ 50,000 resulting in interest of $ 1,500

3) NP33 = $ 50,000 resulting in interest of $ 1,125

4) NP32 = $100,000 resulting in interest of $ 1,166

5) NP31 = $ 50,000 resulting in interest of $ 291.66

In this example, the school district could have earned a total of $15,540.66 in interest. However, even this interest is not the maximum the district could earn. The determination of an optimal investment strategy is similar to solving a complex puzzle, with a prize of additional interest earnings.

While the development of a cash flow chart and the long-term strategy of borrowing and investing of funds for the fiscal year (cash budgeting), is a major component of sound financial management operation in a school district, there is a second component that is equally as important: working capital management. Working capital management is concerned with the day-to-day financial operations of a district. In this process, cash is usually found in either the checking accounts of the district, or in short-term interest bearing assets such as a savings account or repurchase agreement. Cash is transferred from a checking account to a savings account when not immediately needed. Thus, cash is treated as a stock of an inventory good. As such, cash may be manipulated by many of the same techniques that are used in inventory control. The use of two cash management techniques, the Baumol Model and the Miller-Orr Model, are based on this inventory theoretic approach to cash management. These techniques are beyond the scope of this Handbook. Interested readers should look to Dembowski, 1981.

School Banking Relations

School districts have been relatively lethargic concerning their banking business. Studies have shown that:

* most school districts make use of only one bank for all their banking needs;

* many school districts do not use savings accounts;

* the majority of districts do not bid for banking services but select their commercial bank haphazardly;

* school business officials do not know why they are being assessed an annual fee for banking services or how that fee is derived; and

* few business officials realize that there is a minimum or minimum average cash balance requirement with a district's depository account to compensate a bank for its service.

School districts have always been favored customers of commercial banks for a number of reasons: An officer of a local bank is often a member of the local school board, or, less frequently, the superintendent of schools is on the board of trustees of a local bank. Handling school district funds is advantageous to a bank for, as the manager of a commercial bank stated, "When other depositors know that a school district maintains all of its accounts in a bank, they feel that the bank must be very 'safe' because school districts are very careful with their money." School district accounts are likely to be among the largest accounts that a bank handles, especially in rural areas. In addition to the volume of funds that flows through a bank, a school district typically maintains large cash balances in its depository accounts. For these reasons, banks have traditionally sought out school district business.

Different banks use different methods of determining the profitability of the accounts they service. The methods of "profitability analysis" used by banks change over time. Each cash manager should determine how his depository bank conducts its analysis and how his district may use the bank's method to its best advantage. The method outlined here was derived from a case study of a school district in upstate New York. The school district maintained relations with one bank for its checking and savings accounts. It used the same bank to invest money in Certificates of Deposit and other securities. The school district made all payments to employees and vendors by check. The bank incurred expenses - primarily labor costs - in servicing these accounts. These expenses were for services, such as check reconciliation, accepting deposits and check clearing. Banks are usually recompensated for these expenses by requiring that a minimum or minimum average daily cash balance be maintained in a checking account and/or by charging an annual fee.

In determining how much of a fee to charge or at what level to set the compensating balance requirement, a bank performs a "profitability analysis" to determine the expenses of servicing an account for a period of time. For the sample school district in this example, the total expenses of banking for a five-month period were:

An Overview

Number of checks: 17,646 at $.10..............................$1,764.60

Number of deposits: 6,094 at $.05................................304.70

Fixed monthly charge...10.00

Stop payment requests: 11 at $4.00................................44.00

Master Charge sales: 208 at $.95.................................197.60

Check reconciliation..219.69

Total Expenses...$2,540.59

    Once the bank estimated these charges or expenses for servicing the school district's accounts, it then determined whether there is a net profitability for the bank by calculating the earnings allowance of the accounts. The earnings allowance of the accounts accrues to the bank because the money sitting in the checking account may be partially invested by the bank in interest earning assets. The earnings allowance on these accounts is determined as follows. First, the bank records showed that for the five-month period in question, the gross average daily cash balance in the school district's accounts was $359,200. In order to meet governmental liquidity requirements and other technical problems, the bank stated that only 75 percent of this cash balance was available to the bank for investment purposes. Thus, the bank could invest $269,400 of the $359,200. The bank then stated that it could earn only 2.4 percent annual interest on its investments of these funds. Thus, for the five-month period under analysis, the bank determined that it could earn $2,694.22 in interest on the school district checking account ($269,400 x 5/12 x .024 = $2,694.22). The net profitability of the checking account is equal to the interest earnings minus the account expenses ($2,694.22 - $2,540.59 = $153.63). Thus, the bank would be making a profit of $153 for the five months or $367 annually. In addition to this profit, the bank was also charging the sample school district $870 annually as a fee for banking services, resulting in a total profit to the bank of $1,237 annually after expenses.

    The bank's profitability analysis is unfavorable to a school district with built in biases for a particular bank. In the example cited above, the bank did not explain how its charges for various services provided to the school district were determined, other than stating that the charges were "standard" prices charged by most banks. Further, the bank did not justify its earnings allowance determination of only being able to invest 75 percent of the cash balances of the district, and being able to earn only 2.4 percent annual interest on investments. While it is true that a bank may not be able to invest the entire amount available for a variety of reasons, a bank can certainly invest at a rate higher than 2.4 percent annual interest. Even if the funds are invested at the U.S. Treasury Bill rate, a bank could earn substantially higher interest.

A school district could do a number of things to prevent a detrimental situation with its bank. First, when selecting a bank, a school district should solicit bids or request proposals for banking services at the lowest cost. Another alternative is to discuss the account analysis procedures with a number of banks before making a selection. However, the most important thing that a cash manager should do in this situation is to ensure that the district's cash balances remain low by investing excess cash from checking accounts in interest bearing assets. Many business officials feel constrained by the compensating balance requirement set by a bank, and leave cash in a checking account well over this amount.

However, there will always be excess cash in a checking account because of the "float". Float is a term used to describe the amount of cash that remains in a checking account after checks have been written and the checks clear the account. In school districts, the float is typically large, often reaching $50,000 to $100,000. A sound cash management procedure would be to determine this float, and then leave sufficient cash in the checking account over this amount to cover the bank's compensating balance requirement. By this method, a district could invest the remainder of its cash balances in interest bearing assets, earning higher rates of interest. If the sample school district in the example above used this method, it could have earned a minimum of 5 percent of approximately $250,000 or $12,500 at no cost to the district by placing excess funds in a savings account. In addition to this process, school districts should consider the use of "zero balance" account services offered by many banks.

To facilitate this type of cash management, a school district could take advantage of additional banking services. Most banks offer telephone transfers of cash between checking and savings accounts, although this method of cash management has been made somewhat obsolescent by the introduction of NOW accounts.

If a business official calls the bank on a daily basis to determine what the checking account balance is, a decision can be made on whether to transfer cash from a savings account to checking or vice versa. This decision would be made based upon the checking balance, the amounts of outstanding checks and the daily cash needs of the district. Only the amount of cash required to meet the immediate cash expenses of the district need be left in a checking account.

An Overview 37

The remainder should be transferred to interest-bearing assets. This transfer system may be facilitated through the use of a computerized cash management system that many major banks are now offering (such as the CHEMLINK system offered by Chemical Bank). Accordingly, all daily cash receipts should be placed in interest bearing accounts. All large cash deposits, such as state aid payments and tax receipts should be placed directly into interest bearing assets. The daily interest earnings on $1 million in a 5.25 percent savings account is $144.00. Many school districts leave this cash in a checking account over night while deciding what to do with it. Instead, it could be earning additional interest for the district. Through the use of a telephone transfer or computerized cash management system, a school district, and not a bank, would have control over the interest earning assets of the district.

Another service offered by banks that is not used by school districts is the commercial line of credit. This method of financing is often prohibited by law. However, in states where the practice is not prohibited, school districts should consider its use. If the practice is now prohibited, school districts should lobby for enabling legislature for its use.

Lines of credit offer an overdraft protection to school districts that is now being met by leaving excessively large cash balances in accounts as a margin of safety. This margin of safety is costing taxpayers thousands of dollars annually in lost interest revenues. Through the use of lines of credit, a bank lends a school district cash as needed to cover overdrafts. The loan would be at a specified rate of interest, payable when the overdraft is covered. Because the bank would be loaning cash to a tax-exempt institution, the rate of interest is likely to be low, perhaps as low as 8 percent annually. Since many long-term investments have interest rates much higher than this, any cash left in checking accounts as protection against overdrafts could be invested in securities earning substantially higher interest revenues. With a daily monitoring system of checking balances such as described here, the chance of overdrafts would be minimized. Any overdrafts that did occur could easily be paid from the interest earnings on investments made from the cash previously left in the accounts to protect against overdrafts. While the use of credit lines such as described above is prohibited by statutory law in many states, enabling legislation should be lobbied for by school districts.

Summary

Very few school districts now use all of the financial methods suggested in this overview. In fact, it is likely that most school district cash managers do not even know that their bank has a minimum compensating balance requirement, probably because their cash balances have been historically so high that the bank has had no reason to tell the school district about the requirement. As school districts become more sophisticated in cash management, there will be a movement of cash out of the checking accounts into interest bearing assets. This will reduce the average daily cash balances in the depository accounts, forcing banks to set new cash balance requirements or annual banking fees. School business officials should be aware of what is happening and take an active role in this process. In the future, cash management will play an increasingly important role in the financial picture of school districts.

SECTION II

SCHOOL DISTRICT FINANCIAL MANAGEMENT PRACTICES

THIS section reports on a survey of the cash management practices of school districts in the 50 United States sponsored by the Association of School Business Officials in the United States and Canada. The intent of the study was to compile information regarding school district investing practices and borrowing and banking relations in each of the states with a focus on the governance of those financial management operations.

A questionnaire was developed (see Appendix A) with a primary focus on the statutes, regulations and opinions that authorize and limit cash management practices in the states. This questionnaire was sent to the Chief State School Officer in each state. That person was asked to pass the questionnaire on to the official in the state responsible for school district financial management practices. Included with the questionnaire was a return self-addressed stamped envelope to facilitate easy response to the questionnaire. To ensure a high response rate, follow-up telephone calls and letters were sent to all non-respondees within a six-week time period.

The Survey Instrument

The questionnaire was divided into four principal sections. The first asked for general information including a check list of the laws, regulations and opinions which govern financial management in that particular state. The section also included the number of school districts in the state and the total earnings on investments for the state for the 1979-80 school year.

The second section asked questions about school district investing and focused on the sources of funds for investment, the securities that may be used for investment and particular issues concerning investments such as collateral requirements, limitations on the length and amounts of investments and other investment opportunities.

The third section of the questionnaire was principally concerned with school district borrowing including questions concerning borrowing obligation instruments, time and amount limitations for borrowing and some questions concerning arbitrage and reinvestment of the proceeds of borrowed obligations.

The fourth and final section of the questionnaire was concerned with school-banking relationships, and focused on the type of financial institutions school districts may develop depository relationships with and the kinds of services that school districts may use.

The remainder of this section provides a summary and analysis of the responses to the questionnaire on school district financial management.

Survey Results

Because school district financial management operations are very strictly controlled and regulated by statutory law and other state regulations, the first question concerned the various types of regulation or laws which restrict school district financial management operations in each of the states. Exhibit VI provides information on the sources of regulations for school district financial management. The table shows six different sources of regulations and the number of states which reported that kind of regulation. As seen from the table, most state regulations (43) are primarily in the Education Law. The second most prevalent source of regulation for school district financial management operations were the Chief State School Officer's Regulations followed by both regulations in the Municipal Law and Comptrollers and Auditors Regulations and Opinions. All states had at least one source of regulation and 30 states had two or more sources of regulations which govern school district financial management operations.

The interest earnings reported by this survey totaled $1.1786 billion. Exhibit VII shows the reported interest earnings and yield on a state-by-state basis. From this table it can be seen that the highest net earning was in the state of Texas: $218.3 million for a net yield of 5.64 percent of total expenditures for K-12 education in 1979-80. Texas was followed by Pennsylvania ($123.7 million for a net yield of 2.78 percent) and New York ($103.8 million for a net yield of 1.34 percent). Many of the states did not report their interest earnings. In some states, school districts are not able to invest monies except through the town or county treasurer, and any interest earnings are not available or not recorded. The average net yield as a percent of total expenditures for the states' reporting investment earnings was 2.264 percent. If all the states in the United States were able to earn 2.264 percent net yield in the 1979-80 school year, the total interest earnings in all 50 states for investment of school district funds would have amounted to more than $1.54 billion (total expenditures of $68.07 billion reported by the survey times the average net yield in 1979-80 of 2.26 percent). The figure each year, of course, would fluctuate with prevailing interest rates.

The second section of the questionnaire was concerned with school district investing practices. The first questions in this section dealt with the sources of funds that can and cannot be invested. Exhibit VIII records the sources of funds invested by school districts and the number of states which can and cannot invest these funds. As seen from that table, the General Fund is the most highly invested fund. However, ten states are not able to invest their general funds. These states are those, again, in which the financial

Financial Management Practices 41

EXHIBIT VI

SOURCES OF REGULATIONS FOR

SCHOOL DISTRICT FINANCIAL MANAGEMENT

Source	Number of States
Education Law	43
Municipal Law	12
County Law	4
Local Finance Law	9
Chief State School Officers Regulations	14
Comptrollers Regulations	12

EXHIBIT VII

INTEREST EARNINGS AND YIELD BY STATE

State	Interest Earning 1979-1980 (in $ millions)	Total K-12 Expenditure (in $ millions)	Percent Net Yield
Alabama	NA	1,089.1	--
Alaska	4.1	NA	--
Arizona	34.9*	767.2	4.55
Arkansas	12.0	529.1	2.27
California	NA	8,245.3	--
Colorado	30.5	1,139.5	2.68
Connecticut	NA	1,158.5	--
Delaware	1.1	213.7	0.51
Florida	64.5	2,598.4	2.48
Georgia	44.8	NA	--
Hawaii	NA	253.5	--
Idaho	10.0	268.1	3.73
Illinois	95.0	NA	--
Indiana	37.7	1,520.0	2.48
Iowa	17.1	1,138.4	1.50
Kansas	NA	810.0	--
Kentucky	12.7	715.2	1.78
Louisiana	34.5	1,172.6	2.94
Maine	1.1	325.5	0.34
Maryland	NA	1,474.5	--
Massachusetts	NA	2,528.2	--
Michigan	80.5	3,571.7	2.25
Minnesota	55.0	1,557.0	3.53
Mississippi	5.6	560.7	1.00
Missouri	4.0	1,366.2	0.29
Montana	5.4	331.0	1.63
Nebraska	13.1	488.2	2.68
Nevada	11.7	240.4	4.87
New Hampshire	0.5	259.0	0.19
New Jersey	NA	3,145.0	--
New Mexico	13.1	457.5	2.86
New York	103.8	7,732.0	1.34
North Carolina	6.4	1,823.5	0.35
North Dakota	NA	189.1	--
Ohio	12.3	3,470.0	0.35
Oklahoma	10.5	844.0	1.24
Oregon	22.0	852.5	2.58

EXHIBIT VII (Continued)

INTEREST EARNINGS AND YIELD BY STATE

State	Interest Earning 1979-1980 (in $ millions)	Total K-12 Expenditure (in $ millions)	Percent Net Yield
Pennsylvania	123.7	4,455.0	2.78
Rhode Island	NA	300.4	--
South Carolina	15.2	752.5	2.02
South Dakota	6.0	220.0	2.73
Tennessee	NA	960.1	--
Texas	218.3	3,872.3	5.64
Utah	20.0	470.6	4.25
Vermont	NA	165.7	--
Virginia	NA	1,781.0	--
Washington	NA	1,492.6	--
West Virginia	14.0	579.7	2.42
Wisconsin	33.4	NA	--
Wyoming	4.1	186.9	2.19

EXHIBIT VIII
SOURCES OF INVESTED FUNDS

Fund	Total Number of States Can Use	Cannot Use
General	40	10
School Store	31	19
School Lunch	35	15
Special Aid	30	20
Debt Service	38	12
Capital Projects	37	13
Trust and Agency	32	18
Public Library	21	29
Bond Proceeds	37	13
Reserve Fund	33	17
Other Funds	14	36

Financial Management Practices   45

management operations of the school districts are assumed primarily by the town and county within which a school district is located. As shown in Exhibit VIII, a wide variety of sources of funds in school districts may be invested and there are a number of sources of monies not listed on the table which can also be invested.

The next two tables, Exhibits IX and X present information on securities used by the states for investment purposes. Exhibit IX indicates that there are at least eight sources of investment securities available to school districts for investment purposes. These include federal and state securities, district and/or municipal securities, Repurchase Agreements, Certificates of Deposit, commercial bank time deposits, savings and loan bank time deposits and NOW accounts. As shown in Exhibit X all sources of investment securities are highly utilized with the exception possibly of district or municipal securities. The most often used investment securities are federal securities, primarily U.S. Treasury Bills, Certificates of Deposits offered by commercial banks and commercial bank time deposits. It is surprising to note that the use of Repurchase Agreements is relatively limited when compared with some of the other investment securities. Exhibit X shows which investment securities are used on a state-by-state basis. As shown in this table, each state differs in the use of these investment securities. In some states school districts are able to use federal securities for investments from all or some of their funds or none of their funds. The key at the bottom of that table provides additional information on whether or not monies from specific funds can be invested in specific securities. For information on a state-by-state basis of investment securities and investment practices, see the individual state summaries in this handbook.

A number of other issues concerning school district investing were also covered by the survey. Exhibit XI lists responses from the 50 states to questions about four specific issues in school district investing:

1) Must investments be secured by collateral as mandated by state law? As shown in Exhibit XI, 24 states require collateral on school district investments. These collateral requirements vary widely across the states. Some states require collateral in an amount exceeding the invested monies. For example, Kentucky requires Certificates of Deposits to be collateralized to the extent of 105 percent of market value by Treasury Bonds or other U.S. Government obligations. Mississippi requires 110 percent collateral for the amount deposited in excess of that insured by the Federal Deposit Insurance Corporation (FDIC) or Federal Savings and Loan Insurance Corporation (FSLIC) regulations.

EXHIBIT IX

INVESTMENT SECURITIES USED IN THE

UNITED STATES

Type of Security	Number of States Can Use	Cannot Use
Federal Securities	41	9
State Securities	33	17
District and/or Municipal	23	27
Repurchase Agreements	31	19
Certificates of Deposit	43	7
Commercial Bank Time Deposits	40	10
Savings and Loan Bank Time Deposits	36	14
NOW Accounts	35	15

Financial Management Practices

47

EXHIBIT X

INVESTMENT SECURITIES USED BY STATE

INVESTMENT SECURITY

STATE	Federal Securities	State Securities	District and Municipal Securities	Repurchase Agreements	Certificates of Deposit	Commercial Bank Time Deposits	S & L Bank Time Deposits	NOW Accounts
Alabama	1	1	1	1	1	1	1	1
Alaska	4	4	4	4	4	4	4	4
Arizona	2	2	2	2	2	2	2	3
Arkansas	1	1	1	1	1	1	3	3
California	2	3	3	3	2	2	3	3
Colorado	1	1	1	1	1	1	1	1
Connecticut	3	3	1	1	1	3	3	1
Delaware	4	4	4	4	4	4	4	4
Florida	2	2	3	1	1	1	1	1
Georgia	1	1	1	1	1	1	1	1
Hawaii	4	4	4	4	4	4	4	4
Idaho	1	1	1	1	1	1	1	1
Illinois	1	1	1	1	1	1	1	1
Indiana	1	1	3	3	1	1	1	1
Iowa	1	3	3	3	1	1	1	1
Kansas	4	4	4	4	1	1	1	4
Kentucky	1	1	1	1	1	1	1	1
Louisana	1	1	3	3	1	1	3	1
Maine	2	2	2	3	2	2	2	2
Maryland	1	1	1	1	1	1	1	1
Massachusetts	1	1	3	2	2	2	2	2
Michigan	2	2	3	2	2	2	2	2
Minnesota	2	2	2	2	2	2	2	2
Mississippi	1	1	1	1	1	1	1	1
Missouri	1	1	3	3	1	1	1	1
Montana	1	3	3	3	1	1	1	3
Nebraska	4	4	4	4	4	4	4	4
Nevada	1	1	1	3	2	3	2	3
New Hampshire	1	1	3	3	1	1	1	1
New Jersey	1	1	1	1	1	1	1	1
New Mexico	1	1	1	1	1	1	1	1
New York	1	1	1	1	1	1	1	1
North Carolina	1	1	1	1	1	1	1	1
North Dakota	1	3	3	3	1	1	3	2
Ohio	1	3	3	1	1	3	3	3
Oklahoma	1	1	1	1	1	1	1	1
Oregon	1	1	1	1	1	1	1	2
Pennsylvania	1	3	3	1	1	1	1	1
Rhode Island	4	4	4	4	4	4	4	4
South Carolina	1	1	1	1	1	1	1	1
South Dakota	1	3	3	1	1	1	1	3
Tennessee	4	4	4	4	4	4	4	4
Texas	1	3	3	1	1	1	1	1
Utah	1	1	1	1	1	1	1	1
Vermont	1	1	1	1	1	1	1	1
Virginia	1	1	1	1	1	1	1	1
Washington	4	4	4	4	4	4	4	4
West Virginia	1	1	1	1	1	1	3	1
Wisconsin	1	1	1	2	1	1	1	1
Wyoming	1	1	3	3	1	1	1	1

Key: 1-used for all funds   2-used for a few funds   3-not used   4-not applicable

EXHIBIT XI

ISSUES IN SCHOOL DISTRICT INVESTING

Issue	Number of States Yes	No
1. Must Investments be secured with collateral?	24	26
2. Are there limitations as to the length and/or amount of investments?	33	17
3. Is "Pooling" allowed?	40	10
4. Can school districts invest with other districts or governmental agencies?	22	28

Financial Management Practices 49

Quite a few states tie their collateral requirement to FDIC or FSLIC insurance regulations. Those states not requiring collateral, however, have restrictions on the amounts of investments up to the maximum of the FDIC or FSLIC insurance requirements.

2) Are there limitations on the length and/or amount of school district investments? As shown in the table, 33 states limit the length or amounts of investments. For example, many states require that all investments mature within the fiscal year in which the investment was made. Another popular limitation is that the investments mature within 90 days of the initial investment. A few states, including New York and Oregon, allow school district investments to go beyond the end of the current fiscal year and limit their maturity to two-year periods. The most prevalent limitation on the amount of an investment is related to the expenditures needed to meet current obligations: school districts can only invest surplus monies over their current expenditure needs.

3) Is pooling allowed? As shown in Exhibit XI, 40 states allow for pooling of accounts to produce larger amounts for investing. In most cases, the larger the investment, the higher the rate of return. However, most states indicate that where pooling is allowed, it is necessary to make sure that interest is pro-rated back into the sources of funds from which an investment was made.

4) Can school districts invest with other districts or governmental agencies? As shown in Exhibit XI, 22 states allow such inter-district or inter-governmental agency investing. A number of states have further facilitated inter-governmental investing by creating investment pools. For example, the state of Georgia has developed the Local Government Pool Act to facilitate this process. In Oregon, the State Treasurer's Office operates an investment pool and New Jersey has developed a state cash management system to help school districts pool investments with other school districts.

The third section of the survey posed questions on issues in school district borrowing. The first question asked for a listing of the kinds of borrowing obligations which are authorized for use in each state. Exhibit XII provides information on six different types of borrowing obligations and the number of states which can and cannot use these obligations. As shown there, the most prevalent instrument or borrowing obligation is the Tax Anticipation Note (TAN), with half of the 50 states being able or authorized to use this type of borrowing obligation. The second most prevalent borrowing obligation is

EXHIBIT XII

USE OF BORROWING OBLIGATIONS IN STATES

Type of Obligation	Number of States Can Use	Cannot Use
Bond Anticipation Notes	23	27
Budget Note	10	40
Capitol Note	13	37
Revenue Anticipation Note	22	28
Tax Anticipation Note	25	25
Other Obligations	12	38

Financial Management Practices 51

the Bond Anticipation Note (BAN). Very few states authorize school districts to use Budget Notes, Capital Notes or other kinds of obligations. One state, Indiana, allows school districts to borrow through holding companies which are set up to finance school building operations. Exhibit XIII shows a state by state summary of the kinds of borrowing obligations school districts are able to use in each state.

As with school district investing, there are a number of unique issues or problems concerned with school district borrowing and banking relations which were explored through this survey. A number of these issues are summarized in Exhibit XIV. The first issue concerning school district borrowing listed on Exhibit XIV deals with the limitations on the payback period. In fact, 36 states had placed limitations on the payback period for school district borrowing. The most common payback period is either within six-months or before the end of the fiscal year. However, a number of states have authorized longer payback periods for particular borrowing obligations such as BANs. For example, in New York State Bond Anticipation Notes, according to survey responses, had a payback period of five years and in Texas, the payback period for Budget Notes and Contract Obligation Notes was reported to be 25 years.

The second question in Exhibit XIV reports on the number of states that place limitations on the amounts that school districts may borrow. As shown there, 41 states had placed limitations on the amount of borrowed funds. These limitations vary according to the kind of borrowing obligation. However, for general borrowing through Tax Anticipation Notes or Revenue Anticipation Notes, 75 percent to 80 percent of the anticipated receipts can be borrowed through these notes.

A few states (such as Colorado) allow the full budgeted amount to be borrowed through either Budget Notes or Revenue Anticipation Notes. However, a few other states may severely restrict the borrowing requirements. For example, Delaware allows only 25 percent of the annual taxes to be collected through the use of the Tax Anticipation Note. In addition, many states have indicated that further authorization is required in order for school districts to borrow funds of any nature.

The third issue concerning school district borrowing listed in Exhibit XIV, is the investment of the proceeds of borrowed funds. 32 states indicated that after school districts had borrowed monies, these monies may be reinvested until needed for their required purpose. The spread between the borrowing rate and the investing rate offers a school district opportunities to earn additional revenues. However, this must be done within the arbitrage limitations placed on school districts by the federal and state governments. In fact, the

EXHIBIT XIII

OBLIGATIONS FOR BORROWING USED BY SCHOOL DISTRICTS

State	Bond Anticipation Notes	Budget Notes	Capital Notes	Revenue Anticipation Notes	Tax Anticipation Notes	Other Obligations
Alabama	N	N	N	Y	N	Y
Alaska	NA	NA	NA	NA	NA	NA
Arizona	N	N	N	N	N	Y
Arkansas	Y	Y	N	Y	Y	N
California	NA	NA	NA	NA	NA	NA
Colorado	N	Y	Y	Y	N	N
Connecticut	Y	Y	Y	Y	N	N
Delaware	Y	N	N	N	Y	N
Florida	Y	N	Y	N	Y	N
Georgia	N	N	N	N	Y	N
Hawaii	NA	NA	NA	NA	NA	NA
Idaho	N	N	N	N	Y	N
Illinois	N	N	N	Y	Y	Y
Indiana	Y	N	N	Y	Y	Y
Iowa	N	N	N	N	N	Y
Kansas	NA	NA	NA	NA	NA	NA
Kentucky	N	N	N	N	Y	N
Louisana	Y	Y	N	Y	Y	N
Maine	Y	N	Y	Y	Y	N
Maryland	NA	NA	NA	NA	NA	NA
Massachusetts	Y	N	N	Y	N	N
Michigan	N	N	N	N	Y	Y
Minnesota	N	N	N	Y	N	Y
Mississippi	N	N	Y	Y	Y	N
Missouri	N	N	N	N	Y	N
Montana	Y	N	N	N	N	Y
Nebraska	NA	NA	NA	NA	NA	NA
Nevada	Y	Y	Y	Y	Y	N
New Hampshire	Y	N	N	N	N	N
New Jersey	Y	Y	Y	Y	Y	N
New Mexico	N	N	N	N	N	N
New York	Y	Y	Y	Y	Y	Y
North Carolina	N	N	N	N	N	Y
North Dakota	Y	N	N	N	Y	N
Ohio	Y	N	N	Y	Y	N
Oklahoma	Y	N	N	N	N	N
Oregon	N	N	N	Y	N	N
Pennsylvania	Y	N	Y	Y	Y	N
Rhode Island	NA	NA	NA	NA	NA	NA
South Carolina	Y	N	N	Y	Y	N
South Dakota	Y	N	Y	Y	N	Y
Tennessee	N	N	N	N	N	N
Texas	N	Y	Y	N	Y	Y
Utah	Y	N	Y	Y	N	N
Vermont	Y	Y	Y	Y	Y	N
Virginia	Y	Y	N	Y	Y	N
Washinton	NA	NA	NA	NA	NA	NA
West Virginia	N	N	N	N	N	N
Wisconsin	N	N	N	N	Y	N
Wyoming	Y	N	N	N	Y	N

Key: Y-Yes   N-No   NA-Not available or not applicable

Financial Management Practices

EXHIBIT XIV

ISSUES IN SCHOOL DISTRICT BORROWING

AND BANKING

Issues	Number of Responses Yes	No (or not applicable)
1. Does your state have limitations on the pay-back period on borrowing?	36	14
2. Are there limitations on the amount of borrowing?	41	9
3. Can the proceeds of borrowings be reinvested until needed?	32	18
4. Does your state have limitations on arbitrage?	9	41
5. Can school districts use out-of-state banks?	23	27

fourth question in Exhibit XIV asked: does your state have a particular limitation on arbitrage? Only nine states indicated that there is a statutory limitation on arbitrage. At best it seems that a large number of states (at least 18) do not take advantage of the opportunity within the Federal Arbitrage Regulation to reinvest borrowed funds and earn additional monies on investments for their school districts.

The final issue dealt with on Exhibit XIV was the use of out-of-state banks by school districts. Only 23 states reported that school districts are able to use out-of-state banks either for depository relationships or borrowing or investing relationships. The majority of states reported require in-state banking relations for school districts.

The final section of the survey asked questions about school/banking relationships. Based on responses to questions in that section, Exhibit XV presents information on the use of different kinds of financial institutions by school districts across the United States. As shown in Exhibit XV, school districts in 44 states are allowed to develop depository relationships with commercial banks. This is the most prevalent financial institution used by school districts for banking purposes. Thirty-six states allow school districts to develop depository relationships with savings and loan banks. Relatively few states allow school districts to develop financial arrangements with either investment firms or private brokers or other kinds of financial institutions.

The final issue dealt with in the survey was the banking services utilized by school districts. Exhibit XVI shows the wide variety of services offered by banks to school districts and the number of states in which school districts can or cannot use these particular services. The most widely used banking services are safety deposit boxes and investment services. Very few school districts are able to use the tax collection services which are offered by many banks. As indicated in Exhibit XVI there are a wide variety of banking services including accounting and auditing functions, direct deposit of payroll, wire and telephone transfers and handling of coin and currency, are offered by banks, but not utilized by school districts in large number of states.

Summary

In the foregoing discussion of the responses to a survey of cash management practices in the 50 United States, it was noted that there is a wide variation in the kinds of borrowing and investing services which school districts are able to engage in. It was also noted that many school districts borrowing and investing practices are severely restricted through statutory laws and/or regulations. It is hoped

Financial Management Practices

EXHIBIT XV

SCHOOL DISTRICT USE OF FINANCIAL

INSTITUTIONS

Type of Institution	Number of States Can Use	Cannot Use
Commercial Banks	44	6
Savings and Loan Banks	36	14
Investment Firms	16	34
Private Brokers	11	39
Other	1	49

EXHIBIT XVI

BANKING SERVICES USED BY SCHOOL DISTRICTS

Type of Service	Number of States	
	Can Use	Cannot Use
Tax Collections	7	43
Lock Boxes	31	19
Safety Deposit Boxes	37	13
Payroll Disbursement	30	20
Check Reconciliation	30	20
Accounting and Auditing	22	28
Direct Deposit of Payroll	28	22
Telephone/Wire Transfers	28	22
Handling of Coin and Currency	28	22
Investment Services	35	15
Other	6	44

Financial Management Practices 57

that the information provided by the responses to a survey in this nature, will be used as food for thought in revising many of the restrictive statutory regulations which govern school district cash management procedures in the 50 states. The following section presents a state-by-state summary of the borrowing and investing practices and banking relations which are authorized by statutory laws or regulations in each state.

SECTION III

STATE-BY-STATE SUMMARY
OF SCHOOL DISTRICT FINANCIAL MANAGEMENT PRACTICES

THIS section contains a summary of the information reported in response to the survey questionnaire discussed in the previous section. The following pages present a state-by-state summary of the financial management practices in each of the 50 United States. Each summary provides the following information, if available and reported:

1) 1979 school districts statistics including the number of school districts, number of K-12 students, total K-12 expenditures, actual or estimated net interest earnings on school district investments and the net yield on investments, calculated by dividing the total interest earnings by total K-12 expenditures.

2) The primary laws or regulations governing school district financial management including summaries of investment practices, borrowing practices and banking practices.

ALABAMA

1979 School District Statistics:

    127 Districts
    746,000 Students
    Total Expenditures: Not Reported
    Investment Earnings: Not Reported

SUMMARY -- School district financial operations are governed by Chapter 13 of Title 16 of the Education Law and numerous Comptroller's opinions.

    Districts can invest cash from all funds. Capital project funds are further regulated by Sec. 16-13-109. Districts may use federal, state, municipal and district securities, as well as repurchase agreements, certificates of deposit, commercial bank time deposits, savings and loan bank time deposits and NOW accounts. Investments do not require collateral, and there are no limitations to the length or amounts of investments. Pooling of accounts and interdistrict investing are permitted. In general, the investing authorization in Alabama is very permissive.

    School districts can borrow cash only through Revenue Anticipation Notes (Sec. 16-13-3 and Sec. 16-13-145) and Warrant Anticipation Notes (Act. No. 79-823). There is no dollar limit on borrowing. The payback limit on revenue anticipation notes is the end of the fiscal year. The payback limit on warrant anticipation notes is 18 months with a reinvestment option of an additional 18 months. The current maximum rate for school district loans is 6%.

    Alabama school districts may use commercial and savings banks, investment firms and private brokers.

State-by-State Summaries

ALASKA

1979 School District Statistics:

    52 Districts
    88,573 Students
    Total Expenditures: Not Reported
    Investment Earnings: $4,160,671

SUMMARY -- Cash management in school districts in Alaska is directly related to the flow of revenues. There are essentially two levels of control (municipal and state), related to school district operations (Sec. 14.12.010). The state provides the preponderance of school revenues to City and Borough school districts, and assures the total support of rural school districts. Payments are made monthly. The net effect is that this system significantly limits the investment options relative to operating funds provided by the state, and obviates the need for many types of controls. Municipal governments also have the right to require combined treasury operations (Sec. 14.14060).

In 1980, the state legislature enacted new provisions into the Alaska Public School Foundation Program which require a minimum expenditure for instruction, and limit the allowable balance of the school operating fund. Each should have the effect of reducing the volume of invested funds.

The management of capital project funds rests almost exclusively with either the municipal government or the state, depending on the type of school district. The school districts in Alaska do not directly manage these funds.

ARIZONA

1979 School District Statistics:

226 Districts
498,000 Students
Total Expenditures: $767,208,000 (K-12)
Investment Earnings: $ 34,855,248 (4.54% yield)

SUMMARY -- Cost management priorities are regulated primarily by the Education Law (ARS 34-325). Arizona school districts can invest all sources of funds including insurance proceeds, unemployment compensation, school plant, crisis center and the community school progress fund, but not federal aid or trust and agency funds. Most funds may be invested in federal and state securities. Only general fund monies may be invested in district or municipal securities. The general fund cost may also be invested in repurchase agreements, certificates of deposit, commercial bank time deposits and savings and loan bank time deposits. NOW accounts may not be used. Securities are required to be collateralized and investments must mature within 12 months. Pooling of funds with the county treasurer is permitted.

Arizona school districts may only borrow cash through a process of warrant registration (ARS 11-634). However, the monies thus received may not be reinvested because they are used to honor outstanding warrants. There are, then, no arbitrage opportunities.

Schools may use either commercial banks or savings and loan banks within the state. All banking services are used except for tax collection and lock boxes.

ARKANSAS

1979 School District Statistics:

374 Districts
446,000 Students
Total Expenditures: $529,000,000
Investment Earnings: $ 12,016,000 (2.27% yield)

SUMMARY -- School district financial operations are regulated primarily by Sec. 13 and 80 of the Education Law. Districts can invest all funds. Sec. 80-728 permits investments in federal, state, municipal and district securities, as well as repurchase agreements, certificates of deposit and commercial bank time deposits as long as securities are backed by collateral in the form of United States government, state or political subdivision bonds or by a security bond. Investments exceeding one fiscal year are not encouraged. Pooling of accounts is permitted. While not prohibited, school districts do not pool investment funds with other school districts.

Districts can borrow through the use of bond anticipation notes, revenue anticipation notes, tax anticipation notes and budget notes, but not capital notes. There are no dollar limits, but payback is usually restricted to the end of the fiscal year. Proceeds may be reinvested with no limitations on arbitrage.

Sec. 13-802 of the Education Law permits school districts to use commercial banks only. Out-of-state banks may be used. Banking services that may be used by school districts are limited to lock boxes, safety deposit boxes and investment services.

CALIFORNIA

1979 School District Statistics:

    1,033 Districts
    4,000,088 Students
    Total Expenditures: $8,245,291,000
    Investment Earnings: Not Reported

SUMMARY -- School district financial operations in California are primarily governed or regulated by the Education Law Secs. 41.015, 41.017 and 41.000 and by the Chief State Officer's Regulations.

    In California, school districts are able to invest their funds through the County Treasurer. Any cash placed in funds may be invested or reinvested by the County Treasurer with the advice and consent of the governing board of the school district. The governing board of any school district which has funds in any special reserve fund or any surplus money that is not required for the immediate use of the school district may invest all the monies in bonds, notes, bills or certificates or other obligations issued by the United States or in bank time certificates, savings and loan deposits or obligations issued by banks for a wide number of federal or state agencies. The investment of money in California school districts is regulated by Sec. 41.015 of the California Education Code.

State-by-State Summaries

COLORADO

1979 School District Statistics:

    181 Districts
    558,000 Students
    Total Expenditures: $1,139,000,000 (K-12)
    Investment Earnings: $ 30,536,000 (2.6% yield)

SUMMARY -- School district financial operations in Colorado are regulated by a number of laws. The Education Law, Titles 22 and 23; the Municipal Law, Titles 24-32; and the County Law, Titles 24-32 provide the main regulation for school district financial operations. In Colorado, school districts are able to invest all funds from all sources of revenue according to Title 24, Sec. 75-601 of the Municipal and County Laws. Further, they are able to invest all their funds in either federal, state, district or municipal securities. They are also able to invest their funds in repuchase agreements, certificates of deposit, commercial bank time deposits, savings and loan bank time deposits and NOW accounts. All investment securities are required to be collateralized and there is no limitation to either the length or the amount of investments. Pooling of accounts to facilitate investments is allowed: school districts are able to invest with other school districts or other local governmental agencies.

    In Colorado, school districts are able to borrow through either warrant notes, revenue anticipation notes or tax anticipation notes. However, they are limited to a six-month payback period and can only borrow to the amount of the budget appropriation. All cash or borrowed monies may be reinvested until needed. There are no limitations on arbitrage opportunities. However, public schools in Colorado are not proper organizations.

    School districts can bank with either commercial banks, savings and loan banks, investment firms or private brokers as long as certain requirements including Federal Deposit Insurance Corporation or collateral pledges are met. Colorado school districts may use all of the banking services offered by local banks except for tax collections.

CONNECTICUT

1979 School District Statistics:

    165 Districts
    587,000 Students.
    Total Expenditures: $1,158,000,000 (K-12)
    Investment Earnings: Not Reported

SUMMARY -- The cash management operations of Connecticut's school districts are regulated by Educational Law, Secs. 10-18 as well as the Local Finance Law in the Town Charter.

Schools may invest funds from the general fund, the special aid fund, the debt service fund as well as bond proceeds and reserve funds. However, they may not invest federal funds or trust and agency funds. School districts are permitted to invest in district and municipal securities as well as repurchase agreements, certificates of deposits and NOW accounts. The investments do not require collateral and there are no limitations to either the length or amount of the investments. Pooling of accounts is not allowed.

In Connecticut, school districts may borrow through the use of bond anticipation notes, budget notes, capital notes and revenue anticipation notes. However, they cannot use tax anticipation notes. Proceeds from borrowed funds may be reinvested until needed. There are no limitations on arbitrage opportunities, but these are not encouraged.

School districts may use commercial banks or savings and loan banks, but may not use investment firms or other private brokers. School districts are also able to use out of state banks for borrowing or investment purposes. School districts may not use tax collection, lock box or safety deposit box. However, they may use payroll disbursement, check reconciliation, direct deposit at payroll, handling of coin and currency and other investment type services.

State-by-State Summaries

DELAWARE

1979 School District Statistics:

    16 Districts
    108,000 Students
    Total Expenditures: $213,747,000
    Investment Earnings: $ 1,061,000 (.49% yield)

SUMMARY -- The financial operations of school districts in Delaware are primarily regulated by the Education Law, Title 14, Chapters 13, 17 and 19 and the State Government Law, Title 29.

In Delaware, the State Government Law, Title 29, Chapter 27, establishes the State Treasurer as the treasurer for all agencies including school districts. This title also requires all funds be deposited with the State Treasurer. The law further requires that the State Treasurer deposit all funds with the Farmer's Bank of the State of Delaware. This thus precludes any investing on the part of the local school districts.

In Delaware, school districts may borrow through the use of bond anticipation notes and tax anticipation notes. However, bond anticipation notes have a payback limit of four years and must be authorized by a referendum. School districts may borrow through tax anticipation notes to a maximum of 29 percent of annual taxes with a payback period of 90 days. All school districts must bank with the Farmer's Bank of Delaware according to Title 29, Chapter 27 of the State Government Law, and they may use only lock boxes and safety deposit boxes in handling coin and currency. Thus, Delaware is very restricted.

FLORIDA

1979 School District Statistics:

    67 Districts
    1,479,000 Students
    Total Expenditures: $2,598,000,000
    Investment Earnings: $ 67,995,000 (2.6% yield)

SUMMARY -- In Florida, school financial operations are primarily regulated by the Education Law, Chapters 236 and 237 of the Florida Statutes and the Auditor's and Comptroller's Regulations, Chapter 11-35 of the Florida Statutes.

    School districts are able to invest money from the general fund, the school lunch fund, debt service, capital projects and bond proceeds. The funds from those various sources may be invested in federal, state or district municipal securities, repurchase agreements, certificates of deposits, commercial bank time deposits and savings and loan time deposits. The funds from the general fund and the school lunch fund may also be invested in NOW accounts. However, collateral is required to secure all investments. Pooling of accounts is allowed to facilitate larger investments. School districts may invest with other school districts or other local governmental agencies.

    School districts in Florida may borrow through bond anticipation notes, revenue anticipation notes or tax anticipation notes. The proceeds from the borrowed obligations may be reinvested until needed. However, Chapter 237.151 limits short-term loans to one year and not to exceed 80 percent of the estimated tax receipts for that year. Chapter 237.161 permits a short-term loan to be extended for up to four years but limits the loan to 25 percent of prior year tax receipts. In no instance may the total of all loans and bond indebtedness exceed 10 percent of the non-exempt tax roll.

    Schools in Florida may use commercial banks, savings and loan banks or investment firms. They are not permitted to use private brokers. Investment firms may only be used for bond sales. School districts may use all services offered by banks except for tax collection. However, any conflicts of interest must be disclosed between school board members and banking officials.

State-by-State Summaries

GEORGIA

1979 School District Statistics:

    187 Districts (159 County and 28 City Districts)
    1,670,000 Students
    Total Expenditures: Not Reported
    Investment Earnings: $34,788,000

SUMMARY -- In Georgia, school financial operations are regulated by the Education Law, Sec. 32-942, the Municipal Law which differs dependent on City Charters and the Chief State School Officer's Regulations as documented in the Georgia Accounting Handbook and the Attorney General's Opinion which are published yearly.

    School districts can invest all funds, except for public library proceeds, in either federal, state or district and municipal securities, repurchase agreements, certificate of deposits, commercial bank time deposits, savings and loan bank time deposits, NOW accounts, prime banker's acceptances and credit union deposit and insurance corporations. Collateral is required for all investments over the excess of those insured by the Federal Deposit Insurance Corporation insurance. Pooling of accounts within a system for investment is encouraged particularly in the state plan. School districts can also invest in other school districts.

    In Georgia, school districts are permitted to borrow through the use of tax anticipation notes but are not able to use bond anticipation notes, budget notes, capital notes or revenue anticipation notes. Tax anticipation note borrowing is limited to 75 percent of the prior year's taxes, and all monies must be repaid by December 31. All borrowed monies may be reinvested until needed.

    Georgia school districts may bank with commercial banks, savings and loan banks, mutual savings banks and credit unions. They may use all services banks provide except for tax collection purposes.

HAWAII

1979 School District Statistics:

    1 District
    Students: Not Reported
    Total Expenditures: Not Reported
    Investment Earnings: Not Reported

SUMMARY -- The Department of Education for the state of Hawaii is unique in that there is only one school district in Hawaii. It is divided into 7 administrative districts. The state legislature appropriates funds for the Department of Education for the operation of the school system. The financial operations of the department are strictly controlled by state statutes; primarily Title V of the State Financial System, Chapters 36, 37, 38, 39, 40 and 41. Thus, all borrowing and investing for the school district is done at the state level. Administrative districts may use either commercial banks or savings and loan banks.

IDAHO

1979 School District Statistics:

    115 Districts
    199,000 Students
    Total Expenditures: $268,000,000
    Investment Earnings: $ 9,958,000 (3.7% yield)

SUMMARY -- The financial operations of school districts in Idaho are primarily governed by the Education Law, Chapters 5 and 7 of Title 33 of the Idaho Code and the General State Law, Chapter 1, Title 57 and Chapter 12, Title 67.

    School districts in Idaho can invest funds from the general, school lunch, special aid, debt service and capital project funds as well as bond proceeds and other reserves in federal, state and municipal securities, repurchase agreements, certificates of deposits, commercial bank time deposits, savings and loan bank time deposits and NOW accounts. School districts are required to secure their investments with collateral. Idle funds may be invested until needed for purposes for which they were collected, thus there is no limitation to the length or amount of investments. Pooling of accounts within school districts is allowed to facilitate larger investments and school districts are able to combine funds with other school districts for investment purposes.

    In Idaho, school districts are allowed to borrow only through the use of tax anticipation notes. This borrowing is limited to 75 percent of the tax levy not yet collected during the fiscal year and is regulated by Sec. 63-3104. The proceeds of the borrowing may be reinvested until needed and there is no limitation on arbitrage opportunities.

    In Idaho, school districts are able to bank with both commercial banks and savings and loan banks, and they can use full services except for tax collection purposes. The statutes for that contain restrictions on banking services.

ILLINOIS

1979 School District Statistics:

    1,013 Districts
    2,050,000 Students
    Total Expenditures: Not Reported
    Investment Earnings: $95,000,000

SUMMARY -- School district financial management operations are governed by the Illinois revised Statute, Chapters 122 and the Chief State School Officers regulations. In Illinois, school districts are able to invest all funds. The investment of these funds is further regulated by Illinois Statutes Chapter 102, Sec. 34, Chapter 85, Secs. 901 through 95 and Chapter 122, Secs. 34 and 28. These statutes allow funds to be invested in federal, state, district and municipal securities, as well as repurchase agreements, certificates of deposit, commercial bank time deposits, savings and loan time deposits and NOW accounts. Districts may also invest their cash in commercial paper. Collateralization is required on all investments. There are no limitations to the length or amounts of investment as long as the school district meets its cash flow needs. These are regulated by Illinois revised Statute, Chapter 85, Sec. 901 through 905. Pooling of accounts to facilitate larger investing amounts is allowed and school districts are allowed to invest with other districts or local governmental agencies.

    School districts in Illinois borrow through the use of revenue anticipation notes, tax anticipation notes, teacher orders, employee wage orders and bonding. School districts are not able to borrow through bond anticipation notes, budget notes or capital notes. There is a two year maximum payback limit on tax anticipation notes and there is a one year payback limit on warrants. Illinois school districts can reinvest cash from borrowed obligations until needed except for monies borrowed through teacher orders and employee wage orders. Many school districts use interfund transfers in lieu of borrowing money from outside firms.

    Illinois school districts are able to use commercial banks, savings and loan banks and investment firms and are able to use a wide variety of banking services. However, the school districts may not use tax collection services offered by banks or auditing services. There are some other limitations in Illinois with regard to school banking relations. These are listed in the <u>Handbook for School Treasurers</u> distributed by Illinois State Education Department.

State-by-State Summaries

INDIANA

1979 School District Statistics:

    304 Districts
    1,087,000 Students
    Total Expenditures: $1,520,000,000 (K-12)
    Investment Earnings (1979-80) $ 37,670,000 (2.48% yield)

SUMMARY -- School district financial management operations in Indiana are regulated primarily by the Indiana Code IC 21-1 through 21-5, and the State Board of Accounts Statutes IC 5-11 and 12-13.

    Districts in Indiana can invest funds from a wide variety of sources including the cumulative building fund and holding corporations. Districts may invest through the use of federal and state securities, certificates of deposit, commercial bank time deposits, savings and loan bank time deposits and NOW accounts. They may also invest in preferred stocks and bonds of a holding company organized for the construction of school buildings within the taxing limit of such school corporations (IC 21-2-8-1). All investments are required to be secured by collateral. There are no limitations to the length or amounts of investments. Pooling of funds is allowed (IC 5-13-1) and school districts can invest with other school districts.

    Indiana school districts can borrow funds through the use of bond anticipation notes, revenue anticipation notes, tax anticipation notes and through holding corporations. The bond anticipation notes have a dollar limit of 2 percent of assessed valuation with a payback period of six months. Both the bond anticipation notes and tax anticipation notes have a dollar limit of 80 percent of the total anticipated funds with a payback limit of six months. However, borrowed funds may not be reinvested.

    School districts in Indiana may develop depository relationships with both commercial banks and savings and loan banks. Out of state banks may be used if a combined capital and surplus of $10 million is shown on the last published report of the bank. A wide variety of banking services may be used except for check reconciliation and accounting and audit services.

IOWA

1979 School District Statistics:

    443 Districts
    555,000 Students
    Total Expenditures: $1,138,000,000
    Investment Earnings (1979-80): $ 17,088,000 (1.5% yield)

SUMMARY -- School districts in Iowa are able to invest funds of all sources including court liability insurance and unemployment compensation. The investment of funds in Iowa is regulated by Chapters 252, 253 and 254 of the Iowa Code and the Attorney General's Opinion, Sec. C-268. Iowa school districts are able to invest funds from a wide variety of sources in federal securities but not in state, district or municipal securities, according to the Iowa Codes, Chapter 452.10. They are able to invest funds in certificates of deposit, commercial bank time deposits, saving and loan time deposits and NOW accounts but not repurchase agreements. Collateralization is not required for investment securities and there is no limitation to their length of time. By resolutions, school boards must designate depository banks, and a maximum deposit in each bank, and certify the maximum deposit and depository banks to the treasurer of the state. Thus, the amounts required to be in the banks restricts the number and amount of investment possibilities.

    School districts in Iowa are able to borrow monies through anticipatory warrants according to Chapter 74 of the Iowa Code. They are able to borrow through anticipatory warrants an amount legally available and believed to be sufficient to cover anticipated deficiencies. Warrants must be repaid when revenue is received. This precludes the opportunity to reinvest borrowed monies and there is no opportunity for arbitrage. School districts are able to use commercial banks and savings and loan banks for depository relationships but not investment firms or private brokers. They are able to use a number of services including lock boxes, safety deposit boxes and direct deposit of payroll. They are not able to use payroll disbursement, check reconciliation, or accounting and auditing services and cannot use wire transfers or coin and currency services.

State-by-State Summaries   75

KANSAS

1979 School District Statistics:

    307 Districts
    433,000 Students
    Total Expenditures: $810,000,000
    Investment Earnings: Not Reported

SUMMARY -- The financial operations of school districts in Kansas are regulated by the Education Law, Chapter 9, Sec. 1402, Chapter 12, Sec. 1675 and Chapter 17, Sec. 5002.

School districts in Kansas may borrow through a wide variety of funds according to Chapter 12, Sec. 1675 of the Kansas Code. School districts may invest in federal securities, certificates of deposit, commercial bank time deposits and savings and loan bank time deposits. However, 70 percent of all district funds must be supported by federally based securities. All investments in excess of $100,000 must be invested for more than 30 days and must be in banks within the school district provided the bank is willing to pay 91-day treasury bill rate.

In Kansas, school districts may borrow funds through a wide variety of instruments and are able to reinvest proceeds from these borrowings in federal securities. Kansas school districts may develop depository relationships with both commercial banks and savings and loan banks and may use banks either in counties in which school districts are located or in adjacent counties. They are also able to use a wide variety of banking services. The Kansas Bankers Association distributes guidelines for investment of vital funds by school districts in a newsletter obtained by the Division of Financial Services, The State Department of Education and the Legislative Research Department.

KENTUCKY

1979 School District Statistics:

    181 Districts
    679,000 Students
    Total Expenditures: $750,000,000
    Investment Earnings: $ 12,700,000 (1.8% yield)

SUMMARY -- School district financial operations in Kentucky are regulated by Education Law, KRS Chapters 157 and 160 and State Board Regulations.

    School districts in Kentucky are able to invest funds from a wide variety of sources as regulated by KRS Chapter 160 in federal and state securities, repurchase agreements, certificates of deposit, commercial bank time deposits, savings and loan bank time deposits and NOW accounts. They are also able to make investments and direct obligations which are 100 percent guaranteed by the U.S. Government which includes agency notes. There are also collateral requirements: on certificates of deposit, 105 percent of market value of treasury bills or other U.S. Government obligations are required on investments; on direct purchase of treasury bills, repurchase agreements, and so on, no collateral is required as the purchase constitutes collateral requirements. There are no specific statuatory limitations on the length or amount of investments. However, a practical limitation on the general fund is one year. On the investment of bond proceeds, the limitation is the construction period and arbitrage regulations. Pooling of accounts is allowed to facilitate larger investments. However, school districts are not able to invest with other school districts or local governmental agencies.

    In Kentucky, school districts are able to borrow only through the use of tax anticipation notes. They may borrow up to 75 percent of uncollected taxes, but the loan must be repaid within the current fiscal year. Monies obtained through borrowing may not be reinvested and arbitrage is not encouraged. In Kentucky, the current maximum interest that can be paid on short-term tax anticipation notes is six percent.

    In Kentucky, school districts are able to develop depository relationships with commercial banks, savings and loan banks, investment firms and private brokers and are able to use a wide variety of banking services.

State-by-State Summaries

LOUISIANA

1979 School District Statistics:

    66 Districts
    797,000 Students
    Total Expenditures: $1,300,000,000
    Investment Earnings: $ 34,457,000 (2.6% yield)

SUMMARY -- In Louisiana, school districts are able to invest cash in federal and state securities, certificates of deposit, commercial bank time deposits and NOW accounts according to a recent Attorney General opinion.

The financial management operations in the State of Louisiana are regulated by Education Law RS 17:99, Municipal Law RS 33:2955, Chapters 39-1271, Chapter 39-551, 554 and 1307 and Attorney General's opinions. The State of Louisiana does have collateral requirements for investments and there are no limitations to the lengths or amounts of investments. Pooling of accounts to facilitate larger investments is allowed as long as proper accounting procedures are in place. There are no other restrictions on investing.

School districts in Louisiana may borrow through the use of bond anticipation notes, budget notes, revenue anticipation notes and tax anticipation notes. In general, they may borrow up to 75 percent of anticipated deficits according to the various notes and there is generally a five year payback period. The proceeds from borrowed obligations may be reinvested and there are no limitations under current state statutes. There are also no limitations on arbitrage opportunities in Louisiana.

School districts in Louisiana may develop depository relationships with commercial banks but not with savings and loan banks, investment firms or private brokers. While there is no prohibition on the use of out of state banks by school districts, there is, currently, no school district in Louisiana which uses an out of state bank. In Louisiana, school districts may use a wide variety of banking services.

MAINE

1979 School District Statistics:

    86 Districts
    240,000 Students
    Total Expenditures: $325,000,000
    Investment Earnings: $ 1,100,000 (.03% yield)

SUMMARY -- School district financial management operations in Maine are regulated by the Education Law, Municipal Law Title 30 of the MRSA and the Local Finance Law Title 20 of the MRSA, as well as the Chief State School Officers Regulations.

    School districts in Maine are able to invest monies from a wide variety of funds in federal, state, district and municipal securities. They are also able to invest their monies in certificates of deposit, commercial bank time deposits, savings and loan time deposits and NOW accounts. They are not able to use repurchase agreements. Collateral requirements are listed in Title 30 Sec. 5051. There are no limitations to the length or amounts of investments as long as the availability of funds for current operations is met. Pooling of accounts to facilitate larger investments is allowed. There is no exclusion for school districts to invest with other school districts or local governmental agencies.

    School districts in Maine are able to borrow through use of bond anticipation notes, capital notes, revenue anticipation notes and tax anticipation notes. They are able to borrow up to the full extent of state and federal aid or taxes according to the appropriate note but must repay these loans within the current fiscal year.

    School districts in Maine may use either commercial banks or savings and loan banks according to Sec. 5051 for a wide variety of banking services including safety deposit boxes, payroll disbursement, accounting and auditing, direct deposit of payroll, telephone and wire transfers, funds, handling of coin and currency and investment services. Other services are not specifically forbidden.

MARYLAND

1979 School District Statistics:

24 Districts
790,000 Students
Total Expenditures: $1,474,000,000
Investment Earnings: Not Reported

SUMMARY -- The school financial management operations in Maryland are regulated by the Education Law, Secs. 5103-5109; provisions in the Municipal Law, the County and Local Finance Law; the Chief State School Officer's Regulations; and State Comptroller's Regulations and Opinions.

School districts in Maryland are able to invest funds from all sources in all securities that are covered under regulations including federal, state, district and municipal securities, repuchase agreements, certificates of deposit, commercial bank time deposits and savings and loan banks time deposits. However, all investment securities are required to be secured by collateral. However, there is no limitation to either the length or amount of the investment. Pooling of accounts to facilitate large investment amounts is allowed as long as the separate identities of the school funds is allowed for. School districts are also able to invest monies with other districts and local governmental agencies.

In Maryland, school districts are able to establish depository relationships with commercial banks. However, it is not clear whether they can use savings and loan banks. They are not allowed to use investment firms or private brokers. They are also allowed to use out of state banks. Once a depository relationship is established with a commercial bank a school district can utilize a wide variety of banking services with the depository bank.

MASSACHUSETTS

1979 School District Statistics:

    436 Districts
    1,055,000 Students
    Total Expenditures: $2,528,000,000
    Investment Earnings: Not Reported

SUMMARY -- School financial operations in Massachusetts are governed by the Education Law, Municipal Law and Local Finance Law.

School districts in Massachusetts are allowed to invest funds from all sources according to Statute Chapter 44, Sec. 555 and 520 in federal and state securities, repurchase agreements, certificate of deposits, commercial bank time deposit and savings and loan deposits. Only monies from the general fund may be deposited in NOW accounts. The state does not require securities to be collateralized. However, there are limitations to the length of investments.

School districts may borrow through the use of bond anticipation notes and revenue anticipation notes. The proceeds from borrowed obligations may be reinvested until needed according to Chapter 44, Sec. 20 of the Massachusetts Code. There are no limitations on arbitrage opportunities.

In Massachusetts, school districts must use only commercial banks. However, they are able to use a wide variety of banking services offered by these banks.

MICHIGAN

1979 School District Statistics:

    574 Districts
    1,008,000 Students
    Total Expenditures: $3,571,000,000
    Investment Earnings: $ 80,000,000 (2.25% yield)

SUMMARY -- The financial management operations of the school districts in Michigan are regulated by the Education Law, School Code of 1976.

Michigan school districts are able to invest funds from the general, debt service and capital projects funds according to the School Code, Chapter 380.123, in federal and state securities, repurchase agreements, certificates of deposit, commercial bank time deposits, savings and loan bank time deposits and NOW accounts. They are also able to use prime rate commercial paper and have no collateral requirements according to statutory law. However, investments in commercial paper are restricted to those that will not mature more than 270 days from the date of purchase. Pooling of accounts is allowed as long as the investment's income earned can be identified and credited to the accounts involved. School districts may not invest with other school districts or local governmental agencies.

In Michigan, school districts may borrow through the use of tax anticipation notes and state aid notes according to Sec. 134.1 and Sec. 380.1225. When using tax anticipation notes, Michigan School Districts may borrow up to a maximum of 50 percent of tax revenues for a maximum payback time of 13 months from the date of issue. The proceeds of both types of notes may be reinvested while not being used.

In Michigan, school districts may use commercial banks, savings and loan banks, investment firms or private brokers. They can use a wide range of banking services except for tax collection services and may also use out of state banks. However, any out of state bank must be authorized to do business in Michigan according to Chapter 380.1221 and 380.1222.

MINNESOTA

1979 School District Statistics:

    438 Districts
    788,000 Students
    Total Expenditures: $1,557,000,000
    Investment Earnings: $ 53,000,000 (3.4% yield)

SUMMARY -- School district financial management operations in Minnesota are governed by the Education Law and Comptrollers and Auditors Regulations and Opinions.

    School districts are able to invest funds from the general, food service, debt service, equipment, trust in agency, bill construction, and transportation funds according to Minnesota Statutes, Chapter 118.12 in federal, state, district or municipal securities, repurchase agreements, certificates of deposit, commercial bank time deposits, savings and loan bank time deposits and NOW accounts. However, all investments are required to be secured by collateral to the extent of a 110 percent of the principle amount. Pooling of funds is allowed to facilitate larger investments and school districts may invest with other districts and local agencies.

    Minnesota school districts are able to borrow money through the use of revenue anticipation notes, tax anticipation notes, warrants, repurchase agreements or written requests of a county to receive in June a 70 percent advance on taxes. When using revenue anticipation notes, school districts are able to receive up to 75 percent of the aid receivable with a payback period of three months after the end of the fiscal year. With tax anticipation notes, they are able to use or receive 50 percent of taxes receivable within a three month payback period into the new fiscal year. Regardless of the instrument used to borrow monies, surplus cash may be reinvested until needed.

    School districts may use commercial banks, savings and loan banks or investment firms. Regardless of the type of bank used, school districts are able to utilize a wide variety of banking services.

State-by-State Summaries   83

MISSISSIPPI

1979 School District Statistics:

   153 Districts
   482,000 Students
   Total Expenditures: $560,000,000
   Investment Earnings: $ 5,600,000 (1% yield)

SUMMARY -- The financial management operations of school districts in the State of Mississippi are governed primarily by the Education Law, basically Title 37 and Title 29.

   School districts in Mississippi are able to invest monies from their general, school lunch, special aid and seven other funds according to Title 37-59-43 in federal, state, municipal and district securities, repurchase agreements, certificates of deposit, commercial bank time deposits, savings and loan bank time deposits and NOW accounts. The state requires all investment securities to be collateralized to the extent of 100 percent for the amount deposited in excess of that insured by the Federal Deposit Insurance Corporation. There is no limitation on the length of investments. However, the amounts of the investments must not exceed the amount covered by the Federal Savings and Loan Insurance Corporation. Pooling of accounts is allowed to facilitate larger investments. However, school districts may not invest with other districts or other local governmental agencies.

   School districts in Mississippi may borrow funds through the use of capital notes, revenue anticipation notes or tax anticipation notes, according to Mississippi Code, Title 37-59 or 37-39. They may not, however, use bond anticipation notes or budget notes. For capital notes, they may not exceed the amount of the two mill levy, and have a payback period of five years. For revenue anticipation notes, there is a dollar limit of 50 percent of taxes collected, and it must be repaid within the current fiscal year. All proceeds of borrowed obligations may be reinvested until needed. There are no limitations except for the federal regulations on arbitrage.

   School districts in Mississippi may use commercial banks, savings and loan banks or investment firms according to Title 37-59-43 and Title 27-105-350. They may use a wide variety of banking services, including lock boxes, safety deposit boxes, check reconciliation, direct deposit of payroll, telephone and wire transfers and investment services.

MISSOURI

<u>1979 School District Statistics</u>:

    552 Districts
    878,000 Students
    Total Expenditures: $1,366,000,000
    Investment Earnings: $ 40,000,000 (2.9% yield)

SUMMARY -- The financial management operations for school districts in the State of Missouri are regulated primarily by the Education Law, Chapters 164, 165 and 166.

    Missouri school districts are able to invest all money from all funds according to Sec. 165.051 in federal, state, district and municipal securities, certificates of deposits and NOW accounts. However, time deposits are limited to 90 days, and all time deposits, certificates of deposits and NOW accounts must be placed in officially selected depositories which agree to provide sufficient collateral for security. The depository must provide security in a sufficient amount to cover the maximum amount on deposit. Open time deposits are limited to 90 days, and no funds may be invested beyond the point in time when they are required to meet the obligation of the district for which they were authorized. Pooling of accounts with other agencies is not legal and school districts may not invest with other school districts or other local governmental agencies.

    In Missouri, school districts may borrow money through the use of tax anticipation notes according to Sec. 165.131 of the Missouri Code. They may borrow up to a maximum of 50 percent of the tax revenue and there is a payback period of six months.

    School districts in Missouri may develop depository relationships with commercial banks and savings and loan banks, and they may use a wide variety of banking services.

MONTANA

1979 School District Statistics:

    469 Districts
    160,000 Students
    Total Expenditures: $331,000,000
    Investment Earnings: $ 5,400,000 (1.6% yield)

SUMMARY -- The financial management operations of school districts in Montana are regulated primarily by the Education Law. School districts in Montana are able to invest funds from a wide variety of sources in treasury notes, district and municipal securities, certificates of deposit, commercial bank time deposits and savings and loan bank time deposits. There are no restrictions or limitations on investments-other than a payback period of 180 days and there are no collateral requirements. Pooling of accounts at both the district and state levels to facilitate larger investing amounts is allowed. However, no school districts can invest with other school districts or local governmental agencies.

    School districts in Montana are able to borrow monies through the use of bond anticipation notes with a payback period of up to 20 years for these notes. The proceeds of borrowing obligations may be reinvested until needed.

    In Montana, all school district monies are kept by the County Treasurer, thus, there is no reason for a school district to develop a depository relationship with a bank.

NEBRASKA

1979 School District Statistics:

    1,062 Districts
    291,000 Students
    Total Expenditures: $488,000,000
    Investment Earnings: $ 13,000,000 (2.7% yield)

SUMMARY -- In Nebraska, school financial management operations are regulated primarily by the Education Law.

    The school districts in Nebraska are able to invest funds from a wide variety of sources. These investments are primarily regulated by Chapter 77, Secs. 2338 and 2363 and Chapter 72, Sec. 1246. School districts in Nebraska are able to invest these funds in a wide variety of securities, including repurchase agreements, certificates of deposit, commercial bank time deposits and federal and state securities. All of these investments are required to be secured by collateral as stated in statute Chapter 77, Sec. 2352. There is no limitation on the length or amounts of investment and pooling accounts is allowed.

State-by-State Summaries

NEVADA

1979 School District Statistics:

    17 Districts
    143,000 Students
    Total Expenditures: $240,000,000
    Investment Earnings: $ 11,671,000 (4.9% yield)

SUMMARY -- In Nevada, school financial management operations are regulated through a number of laws. Primarily, the Education Law, Chapter 354; Municipal and County Laws; Local Finance Law, Chapter 387; Chief State School Officers Regulations, NRS 387.0 and Comptrollers and Auditors Regulations and opinions on Governmental Accounting and Financial Reporting (GAAFR) and National Council on Governmental Accounting (NCGA) Statement 1, as well as the Nevada Tax Commission and Public Investment Law, Chapter 355 of the Nevada Revised Statutes.

    School districts in Nevada are able to invest monies from the general, school store and seven other funds, according to Chapter 355 of the Nevada Revised Statutes in federal, state, district and municipal securities, certificates of deposit, commercial bank time deposits, savings and loan bank time deposits and NOW accounts. Collateralization of investments is not required, and there are no limitations on the lengths or amounts of investments. Pooling of accounts are allowed, and school districts may invest with other state or local governmental agencies.

    School districts in Nevada are able to borrow money through the use of bond anticipation notes, budget notes, capital notes, revenue anticipation notes and tax anticipation notes. There is no dollar limit. However, there is a five year payback period for all borrowed monies and the proceeds of all borrowed obligations may be reinvested until needed.

    School districts in Nevada may develop depository relationships with a wide variety of banking and savings and loans institutions according to Chapter 355 of the Nevada State Code. Nevada school districts are also able to use a wide variety of banking services as provided by Chapter 354 of the Code.

NEW HAMPSHIRE

1979 School District Statistics:

    167 Districts
    169,000 Students
    Total Expenditures: $259,000,000
    Investment Earnings: $ 524,000 (.02% yield)

SUMMARY -- In New Hampshire, the financial management operations of school districts are regulated primarily by the Education Law, Chapters 198 and 197.23 and other state statutes including Secs. 71a and 35, 33 and 32.

    School districts in New Hampshire are able to invest monies from most funds in federal and state securities, certificates of deposit, commercial bank time deposits, savings and loan bank time deposits and NOW accounts. There are no limitations on the length or amounts of investments and pooling of accounts to facilitate larger investments is allowed. School districts may also invest monies with other districts or local governmental agencies.

    School districts in New Hampshire are able to borrow money through the use of bond anticipation notes and there is a two year payback period. The proceeds from bond anticipation notes may be reinvested until needed.

    School districts in New Hampshire may develop depository relationships with both commercial banks and savings and loan banks. However, the State Code, Chapter 197.23 limits the use of out of state banks to those in Massachusetts. New Hampshire school districts frequently use Massachusetts banks for borrowing and investment purposes. The school districts may use a wide variety of banking services available to them.

State-by-State Summaries

NEW JERSEY

1979 School District Statistics:

    614 Districts
    1,036,000 Students
    Total Expenditures: $3,145,000,000
    Investment Earnings: Not Reported

SUMMARY -- The financial management operations of New Jersey school districts are regulated primarily through the Education Law and Comptrollers and Auditors Regulations and Opinions.

School districts in New Jersey may invest funds from a wide variety of sources in federal, state, district and municipal securities, repurchase agreements, certificates of deposit, commercial bank time deposits, savings and loan bank deposits and NOW accounts. However, all investment securities are required to be secured by collateral. There is no limitation on either the length or amount of the investment. However, all investments are determined by analysis of individual school district cash flow needs and patterns. Pooling of accounts to facilitate larger investments is allowed. In New Jersey, there has been an effort to develop a state cash management system in which school districts may invest. Some school districts in New Jersey have voluntarily participated in this new system.

School districts in New Jersey may borrow money through the use of bond anticipation notes, budget notes, capital notes, revenue anticipation notes and tax anticipation notes.

In New Jersey, school districts are able to develop depository relationships with both commercial banks and savings banks. However, there is a limited number of services offered by the banks which school districts may use: safety deposit boxes (as long as they're bonded); payroll disbursement services; and investment services by arrangement with the individual banks.

NEW MEXICO

1979 School District Statistics:

    89 Districts
    272,000 Students
    Total Expenditures: $457,000,000
    Investment Earnings: $ 13,101,000 (2.9% yield)

SUMMARY -- Financial management operations of school districts in New Mexico are regulated by State Law, primarily Chapter 21-1-1 through Chapter 22-25-10 of the New Mexico Statutes.

    School districts in New Mexico are able to invest monies from a wide variety of funds. According to Sec. 22-8-40 of the New Mexico Code, these monies may be invested in federal, state, municipal and district securities, repurchase agreements, certificates of deposit, commercial bank time deposits, savings and loan bank time deposits and NOW accounts. However, all investments are required to be secured by collateral. There is no limitation on the length or amount of investments except to bond funds subject to arbitrage laws. Pooling of accounts to facilitate larger investment amounts is allowed. Because the State of New Mexico provides 85 percent of the general operating funds on a monthly basis, this precludes the need for school districts to borrow.

    School districts in New Mexico are able to develop depository relationships with commercial banks and savings and loan banks, and they are able to use a wide variety of banking services.

NEW YORK

1979 School District Statistics:

739 Districts
1,953,000 Students
Total Expenditures: $7,732,000,000
Investment Earnings: $ 103,770,000 (1.34% yield)

SUMMARY -- In New York, school financial management operations are regulated primarily by the Education Law, Sec. 1604a through Sec. 1723a; Fiscal Law GM 11; Local Finance Law, Sec. 165.00; and Comprtollers and Auditors Regulations and Opinions.

In New York, school districts may invest monies from a wide variety of funds in federal, state, district and municipal securities, repurchase agreements, certificates of deposit, commercial bank time deposits, savings and loan bank time deposits and NOW accounts. However, all investment securities are required to be secured by collateral as specified in Education Law, Sec. 1604a and all investments are required to be paid back within a two year period. Pooling of accounts is allowed to facilitate larger investments and school districts are able to invest with other districts or other local governmental agencies.

School districts in New York State are able to borrow through the use of bond anticipation notes, budget notes, capital notes, revenue anticipation notes, tax anticipation notes and statuatory installment bonds. Each of these instruments has its own unique dollar limitation and payback period. The proceeds of all these bond obligations may be reinvested until needed. There are no specific limitations on arbitrage opportunities.

School districts in New York are able to develop depository relationships with commercial banks and may borrow anywhere within the world. However, they have to invest within State. School districts in New York are also able to use all and any banking services available by their depository bank.

NORTH CAROLINA

1979 School District Statistics:

144 Districts
1,135,000 Students
Total Expenditures: $1,823,000,000
Investment Earnings: $ 6,418,000 (est.) (.35% yield)

SUMMARY -- School financial management operations in North Carolina are regulated by an Education Law, Sec. GS 115-100.1 through 115-100.35.

In North Carolina, school districts are able to invest all funds in a wide variety of investment securities including federal, state, district and municipal securities, repurchase agreements, certificates of deposit, commercial bank time deposits, savings and loan bank time deposits and NOW accounts. Investments are not required to be collateralized. Pooling of funds to facilitate larger investment amounts is allowed. School districts may invest with other districts or other local governmental agencies.

School districts in North Carolina are not able to borrow money, because school debt is normally a debt of the county. However, they may borrow from the State Literary Fund according to State Law, Chapter 115-108.1.

In North Carolina, school districts may develop depository relationships with commercial banks, savings and loan banks and private brokers and may use a wide variety of banking services, except for payroll disbursement and auditing and accounting services.

State-by-State Summaries 93

NORTH DAKOTA

1979 School District Statistics:

    327 Districts
    119,000 Students
    Total Expenditures: $180,000,000
    Investment Earnings: Not Reported

SUMMARY -- Financial management operations of school districts in North Dakota are regulated primarily by the Education Law, Title 21, and Municipal Law.

In North Dakota, school districts may invest funds in federal securities, certificates of deposit, commercial bank time deposits and NOW accounts. However, all investments are required to be collateralized and the investment of surplus funds may be taken into account when making levies for an ensuing year. School districts must be able to reconvert all investments very quickly into cash. Pooling of accounts is allowed to facilitate larger investments. However, school districts may not invest with other school districts or local governmental agencies.

School districts may borrow through the use of bond ancitipation notes and tax anticipation notes. They may borrow through tax anticipation notes the amounts of uncollected taxes and there is a one year payback period. The proceeds of all borrowed monies may be reinvested until needed and there is no limitation on arbitrage.

School districts in North Dakota may develop depository relationships with both commercial banks and savings and loan banks, and they may use a wide variety of banking services except those for tax collection purposes.

OHIO

1979 School District Statistics:

    615 Districts
    2,052,000 Students
    Total Expenditures: $3,470,000,000
    Investment Earnings: $ 12,289,000 (3.5% yield)

SUMMARY -- The financial management operations of school districts in Ohio are regulated by the Education Law, Chapter 33.17 Chief State School Officers Regulations and Auditors and Comptrollers Opinions.

School districts in Ohio may invest monies from a wide variety of funds in federal securities, repurchase agreements or certificates of deposit. The state does require all investments to be secured by collateral and there is no limitation on the length or amount of investments. Pooling of accounts within an individual school district is allowed. However, school districts may not invest with other school districts or local governmental agencies.

Ohio school districts may borrow money through the use of bond anticipation notes, revenue anticipation notes and tax anticipation notes according to Chapter 133. They may borrow up to 50 percent of anticipated collections with a payback period of one year. The proceeds of all borrowed obligations may be reinvested until needed.

School districts in Ohio may develop depository relationships with both commercial banks and savings and loan banks but not with investment firms or private brokers. They are also able to use a wide variety of banking services except for tax collection services and auditing and accounting services.

OKLAHOMA

1979 School District Statistics:

619 Districts
576,000 Students
Total Expenditures: $844,000,000
Investment Earnings: $ 10,518,000 (1.24% yield)

SUMMARY -- Financial management operations of school districts in Oklahoma are regulated primarily by Education Law, Title 62, County Law and the Chief State School Officer's Regulations.

School districts in Oklahoma are able to invest monies according to Title 20-62. They may invest in federal, state, district and municipal securities, repurchase agreements, certificates of deposits, commercial bank time deposits, savings and loan bank time deposits and NOW accounts. The state requires all investments be secured by collateral. There is no limitation on either the length or amounts of investments and pooling of accounts is allowed to facilitate larger investments. There is no statutory authority for school districts to combine their accounts with those of other school districts or local governmental agencies for investment purposes.

School districts in Oklahoma are able to borrow money through the use of bond anticipation notes according to Title 62. They may borrow up to 10 percent of the valuation of a bond and have up to 25 years to repay the bond. All proceeds from borrowed obligations may be reinvested until needed and there is no limitation on arbitrage opportunities.

School districts in Oklahoma may develop depository relationships with commercial banks, savings and loan banks and investment firms. However, they are able to use only a limited number of banking services including payroll disbursement, telephone wire transfers and handling of coins and currency.

OREGON

1979 School District Statistics:

311 Districts
460,000 Students
Total Expenditures: $852,000,000
Investment Earnings: $ 22,000,000 (2.6% yield)

SUMMARY -- In Oregon, the financial management operations of school districts are regulated primarily by the Local Finance Law, Oregon State Statute 294.305 and 294.520.

School districts in the state are able to invest monies from the general, school store, school lunch, special aid, trust and agency funds in a wide variety of investment securities. However, all investments must mature within a two year period. Collateral on the investments is not required. Pooling of accounts to facilitate large investments is allowed and school districts may invest with other local school districts or other governmental agencies. The State Treasurer's Office operates an investment pool for local governments in which school districts may partake.

School districts in Oregon may borrow money through the use of revenue anticipation notes. They may borrow up to 80 percent of anticipated revenues and the payback period is one year. The proceeds of revenue anticipation notes may be reinvested until needed. However, bond receipts must be totally spent within three years of receipt, and 10 percent of bond receipts must be spent within six months of receipt.

School districts in Oregon may develop depository relationships with commercial banks, savings and loan banks, investment firms and private brokers. However, they may only use a limited number of services provided by a bank including payroll disbursement, check reconciliation, direct deposit of payroll and investment services. School districts are nornally required to use depository banks within their own counties which precludes the use of other state banks.

State-by-State Summaries

PENNSYLVANIA

1979 School District Statistics:

    505 Districts
    1,998,000 Students
    Total Expenditures: $4,455,000,000
    Investment Earnings: $ 123,733,000 (2.78% yield)

SUMMARY -- Financial management operations of school districts in Pennyslvania are regulated by Education Law, Article VI of the Pennsylvania School Code and Article 4, Sec. 441 Chief State School Officer's Regulations and Auditors Regulations and Opinions.

    School districts in Pennsylvania are able to invest monies from a wide variety of funds in many types of investment securities. However, all investments are required to be secured by collateral to the extent of 120 percent of the invested amount. There is no limitation on the length or amounts of investments, and pooling of accounts to facilitate larger investment amounts is allowed. However, school districts may not invest with other school districts or local governmental agencies.

    School districts in Pennsylvania are allowed to borrow money through the use of bond anticipation notes, capital notes, revenue anticipation notes and tax anticipation notes. There is no limit on the payback period for bond anticipation notes or capital notes. However, there is a one year payback period for revenue anticipation notes and tax anticipation notes. The proceeds of all borrowed obligations may be reinvested until needed.

    School districts in Pennsylvania may develop depository relationships with commercial banks, savings and loan banks, investment firms and private brokers and may use a wide variety of banking services. They are not allowed to use out of state banks for borrowing or investment purposes.

RHODE ISLAND

1979 School District Statistics:

    40 Districts
    158,000 Students
    Total Expenditures: $300,000,000
    Investment Earnings: Not Reported

SUMMARY -- The school financial management operations in Rhode Island are governed by the Education Law, Title 16-4-1 and Local Finance Law through the Home Rule Charter. There are also applicable provisions in the Chief State School Officer's Regulations and the State Comptroller's Regulations and Opinions.

    School districts in Rhode Island do not invest any of their monies. The state invests all funds for them every six months and the Town Treasurer can invest school monies.

    Rhode Island school districts may borrow through the use of bond anticipation notes as stated in the Education Law, Sec. 45-12-4. Other information on financial management operations of Rhode Island school districts or depository relationships with banks is not available.

State-by-State Summaries

SOUTH CAROLINA

1979 School District Statistics:

    92 Districts
    609,000 Students
    Total Expenditures: $752,000,000
    Investment Earnings: $ 15,206,000 (2% yield)

SUMMARY -- The financial management operations of South Carolina school districts are regulated by State Law, primarily Title 6 of the Local Government Law, Chapters 5-10 through 5-40.

    South Carolina school districts are able to invest funds in federal, state, district and municipal securities, repurchase agreements, certificates of deposit, commercial bank time deposits, savings and loan accounts and NOW accounts. The state of South Carolina does not require investment securities to be secured by collateral, and there are no limitations on the length or amounts of investments. Pooling of accounts to facilitate larger investment amounts is allowed and school districts may invest with other school districts and local governmental agencies. The County Treasurer makes all investments with the local educational agencies. School funds can be reinvested with other agency funds. However, in some counties, the interest earned on school district investments accrues to the county's general fund.

    School districts in South Carolina may borrow through the use of bond anticipation notes, revenue anticipation notes and tax anticipation notes. They are not able to borrow using budget notes or capital notes. Usually, they are able to borrow to the full extent of the bond, revenue anticipation or tax anticipation, and all proceeds from borrowed obligations may be reinvested until needed. In South Carolina the interest that can be paid on borrowed monies has a ceiling which can only be raised by the State Budget and Control Board.

    School districts in South Carolina are able to develop depository relationships with commercial banks and savings and loan banks, investment firms and private brokers. They are able to use a wide variety of banking services once they have developed a depository relationship.

SOUTH DAKOTA

1979 School District Statistics:

    195 Districts
    136,000 Students
    Total Expenditures: $220,000,000
    Investment Earnings: $ 6,000,000 (2.7% yield)

SUMMARY -- School financial management operations in South Dakota are primarily regulated by the Education Law, Secs. 13-16-15 through 18 and Sec. 4-6.8-1.

    School districts in South Dakota are able to invest funds from a wide variety of sources in federal securities, repurchase agreements, certificates of deposit, commercial bank time deposits and savings and loan time accounts. All investment transactions in South Dakota shall be by resolution of the board. The same resolution shall be regularly followed and recorded with the business manager as public record. School districts are required to secure their investments by collateral and the collateral must have a value of at least equal to the maximum liability of the investment. There is no limitation on the length or amounts of investments. Pooling of accounts to facilitate larger investments is allowed. However, school districts are not able to invest with other school districts or other local governmental agencies.

    School districts in South Dakota are able to borrow funds through the use of bond anticipation notes, capital notes, revenue anticipation notes and an installment purchase with a maximum of ten years. Using revenue anticipation notes, school districts may borrow up to 95 percent of the levy of a fiscal year.

    School districts in South Dakota may develop depository relationships with commercial banks, savings and loan banks and investment firms. However, they are severely limited in the use of the banking services which they are able to utilize. A few of the banking services they are allowed to use include safety deposit boxes and investment services.

TENNESSEE

1979 School District Statistics:

    148 Districts
    852,000 Students
    Total Expenditures: $960,000,000
    Investment Earnings: Not Reported

SUMMARY -- Under Tennessee law, a local school district board of education is an agency of the local government and, as such, is under the fiscal control of the local legislative bodies such as the County Commission or City Council.

School board funds are deposited with a fiscal agent, usually an elected official of the local government and are invested by him and not by the school board. Earnings from these investments are under the control of the local legislative body and the use of such earnings are determined by the body except that the earnings for bond funds must be accrued to the capital project or be used to retire the debt.

Local school boards may not borrow funds. The local legislative body may authorize the chief executive officer to borrow short term funds for the benefit of local government agencies, or may issue general obligation bonds for capital projects such as school buildings.

The above statements apply to city and county school systems. In addition, there were (when this survey was conducted) 16 special school systems in Tennessee which have been created by the state legislature through private acts. The fiscal procedures for each of these districts is set out in the act in which it was created and those procedures vary from system to system.

TEXAS

1979 School District Statistics:

    1,103 Districts
    1,199,000 Students
    Total Expenditures: $3,872,000,000
    Investment Earnings: $ 218,000,000 (est.) (5.6% yield)

SUMMARY -- School district financial management operations in Texas are primarily regulated by the Education Law and the Texas Education Code, Chapter 23.

    School districts in Texas are able to invest funds from a wide variety of sources, primarily regulated by Texas Code, Chapter 23.77. Texas school districts are able to invest these funds in federal, state, district and municipal securities, repurchase agreements, certificates of deposit, commercial bank time deposits, savings and loan bank time deposits and NOW accounts. Repurchase agreements may be used as provided for by a depository bank form to assist a district in any permitted investments as per Chapter 20.77 of the Texas Education Code. NOW accounts may not be offered by all depository banks. Reserves of bond proceeds set aside to meet construction and project obligations may not be placed in savings and loan accounts. Time deposit open accounts are used on short term investments without the use of supporting paper.

    All investment securities must be secured by collateral. The total funds placed in any and all savings, NOW accounts and demand deposit accounts of depository banks must be 100 percent secured by a pledge of acceptable federal, state, district or municipal securities minus the Federal Deposit Insurance Corporation coverage. Funds may not be invested in savings and loan associations in excess of the Federal Savings and Loan Deposit Insurance Corporation coverage. Funds may be invested for as long as they are not needed for the purpose intended. While the pooling of funds by a school district is not covered by any legislated act, it is done and the earnings of the pooling are distributed on a pro rata basis to the various sources of money. School districts are not able to invest with other school districts or local governmental agencies.

    School districts in Texas are able to borrow money from a wide variety of sources including budget notes, capital notes, tax anticipation notes, time warrants, contract obligation notes and delinquent tax notes. Each of these particular notes has a unique dollar limit and payback period. It is suggested that the various codes, primarily Sec. 20.51, .46 and .49 of the Texas Education Code, be examined for the particular dollar limit and payback period for each borrowing obligation. The investment of borrowed monies is not covered by law. However, the investment of cash as available would be feasible so long as it is not needed for the purpose intended.

TEXAS (Continued)

School districts in Texas may develop depository relationships with both commercial and savings and loan banks. The use of investment firms and private brokers is not authorized. Once a depository relationship is developed, a Texas school district is able to use a wide variety of banking services. However, school districts are not able to use tax collection, payroll disbursement or direct deposit of payroll services.

UTAH

1979 School District Statistics:

    40 Districts
    317,000 Students
    Total Expenditures: $470,000,000
    Investment Earnings: $ 20,000,000 (est.) (4.3% yield)

SUMMARY -- The school district financial management operations in the state of Utah are primarily regulated by the Education Law, the Utah Code, Chapter 53-7-9-10 and -20 as well as the Chief State School Officer's Regulations, the Comptrollers and Auditors Regulations and Opinions with various pronouncements and by the State Money Management Act of 1974 as listed in the Utah Code 51-7-1 through 51-7-21.

    School districts in Utah are able to invest funds from a wide variety of sources in all legal investment securities including federal, state and municipal securities, certificates of deposit, commercial bank time deposits, savings and loan bank time deposits and NOW accounts. However, all investments must be federally secured or insured. In addition, real estate mortgages secured by FAHA insurance loans and loans to college students guaranteed or insured by the U.S. Government are additional securities which may be used for school district investments. There are no limitations on the length or amounts of the investment. However, not more than 20 percent of invested funds may be invested outside of the state. Pooling of accounts is allowed and school districts may invest monies with other districts or local governmental agencies.

    School districts in Utah may borrow through the use of bond anticipation notes, revenue anticipation notes and tax anticipation notes. With each of these, school districts may borrow up to the full dollar limit of the expected value of the bond. The payback period for bond anticipation notes is five years, and all borrowing revenue anticipation notes and tax anticipation notes have to be paid back within the current year. The proceeds of all borrowed obligations may be reinvested until needed.

    School districts in Utah are able to develop depository relationships with commercial banks, savings and loan banks and investment firms and are able to use out of state banks as long as not more than 20 percent of the total investments are with out of state banks. In addition, they are able to use a wide variety of banking services offered by their depository banks.

State-by-State Summaries 105

VERMONT

1979 School District Statistics:

    236 Districts
    99,000 Students
    Total Expenditures: $166,000,000
    Investment Earnings: Not Reported

SUMMARY -- School financial management operations in Vermont are primarily regulated by the Education Law, Title 16, Chapter 7 through 131 and the Chief State School Officer's Regulations.

    School districts in Vermont are able to invest monies from a wide variety of funds in federal, state, district and municipal securities, repurchase agreements, certificates of deposit, commercial bank time deposits, savings and loan bank time deposits and NOW accounts. The state does not require investments to be secured by collateral. However, all investments must mature within the fiscal year. Pooling of accounts to facilitate larger investment amounts is allowed and school districts are able to invest with other districts or local governmental agencies.

    School districts in Vermont may borrow money through a wide variety of instruments including budget anticipation notes, budget notes, capital notes, revenue anticipation notes and tax anticipation notes. However, each of these has a unique dollar limit and the payback period is usually within the current fiscal year. Proceeds of all borrowed obligations may be reinvested within the given time constraints of when the money is needed.

    School districts in Vermont are able to develop depository relationships with commercial banks, savings and loan banks and investment firms. They are able to develop banking relationships with out of state banks within given political constraints. They are also able to use a wide variety of banking services from their depository and other banks.

VIRGINIA

1979 School District Statistics:

131 Districts
1,030,000 Students
Total Expenditures: $1,781,000,000
Investment Earnings: Not Reported

SUMMARY -- School financial management operations in Virginia are primarily regulated by the Education Law, Title 22.1, Municipal Law and County Law, Chapter 15.1, and Chief State School Officer's Regulations and Comptroller's Regulations and Opinions.

School districts in Virginia are not able to invest monies from many sources. They are able to invest monies from school store and other school activity funds. Because of this, the interest earnings available on investments is very limited.

School districts in Virginia are able to borrow monies through the use of bond anticipation notes, budget notes, revenue anticipation notes and tax anticipation notes. They are able to reinvest the monies from borrowed obligations until they are needed.

School districts in Virginia are able to develop depository relationships with commercial banks, savings and loan banks, investment firms and private brokers. They are also able to use a wide variety of banking services with the exception of tax collection and payroll disbursement.

WASHINGTON

1979 School District Statistics:

  300 Districts
  751,000 Students
  Total Expenditures: $1,492,000,000
  Investment Earnings: Not Reported

SUMMARY -- School financial management operations in Washington state are primarily regulated by the Education Law.

Schools districts in the state are not able to invest funds because the County Treasurer invests individually or collectively collected funds. School districts are able to borrow money through the use of bond anticipation notes, warrants and conditional sales contracts. Further information on the financial management operations in the state of Washington is unavailable.

WEST VIRGINIA

1979 School District Statistics:

    55 County Districts
    387,000 Students
    Total Expenditures: $580,000,000
    Investment Earnings: $ 14,000,000 (2.4% yield)

SUMMARY -- School district financial management operations in the state of West Virginia are primarily regulated by the Education Law and the School's Law of West Virginia.

    School districts in the state are able to invest funds in a wide variety of sources according to the School Law, Chapter 18-9-6 and are able to invest funds which are in excess of cash demands in federal, state, district and municipal securities (as long as they are guaranteed by the federal or state governments) and repurchase agreements, certificates of deposit, commercial bank time deposits and NOW accounts. The state does require all invested securities to be secured by collateral which includes adequate bonding, federal and state guarantees and other regulations as stated in the state's Education Law, Chapter 18-9-6. There are no limitations on either the length or amount of investments. Pooling of accounts to facilitate larger investment amounts is allowed.

    School districts in West Virginia are not authorized to borrow. They are able to develop depository relationships with commercial banks and can use a wide variety of banking services with the exception of tax collection purposes. They are also able to use out of state banks for investment purposes.

State-by-State Summaries

WISCONSIN

<u>1979 School District Statistics</u>:

    433 Districts
    865,000 Students
    Total Expenditures: Not Reported
    Investment Earnings: $35,350,000

SUMMARY -- School district financial management operations in Wisconsin are regulated by the Education Law, Chapters 25, 74, 34, 115, 121, 120, 67, 66 and 65, the Municipal Law, Chapters 65-67 and Chapter 74 and the Chief State School Officer's Regulations which prescribe the fund accounting system and the Comptroller and Auditor's Regulations and Opinions used to regulate funds.

    School districts in Wisconsin are able to invest monies from a wide variety of funds in federal, state, district and municipal securities, certificates of deposit, commercial bank time deposits, savings and loan bank time deposits and NOW accounts. Only funds from capital projects can be invested from repurchase agreements. Wisconsin requires school district investment securities to be secured by collateral. Long-term debt is secured by irrepayable taxes and temporary funding of delinquent taxes is secured by tax sales certificates. The time limitations for investments are not more than one year or during the current fiscal year. Pooling of accounts is allowed to facilitate larger investment amounts. However, debt service funds from Fund 30 and building fund, Fund 40, must be held in separate and distinct funds. Other funds may be full. School districts are able to invest with other districts or local governmental agencies.

    School districts in Wisconsin are able to borrow money only through the use of revenue anticipation notes and tax anticipation notes. They are able to borrow up to 50 percent of operation and maintenance receipts. The payback period is by November 1 of the following fiscal year. They are able to reinvest funds from borrowed obligations until needed.

    School districts in Wisconsin are able to develop depository relationships with both commercial banks and savings and loan banks and are able to use a wide variety of banking services with the exception of wire transfer of funds.

WYOMING

1979 School District Statistics:

    39 Districts
    93,000 Students
    Total Expenditures: $187,000,000
    Investment Earnings: $ 4,100,000 (2.2% yield)

SUMMARY -- School district financial management operations in Wyoming are regulated primarily by the Education Law, Chapter 21-13-101 through 21-13-1721, Municipal Law, primarily Chapter 9-2 and the Constitutional State of Wyoming, Chapters 9 through 9-551 through 600.

    The school districts in Wyoming are able to invest monies from a wide variety of sources in federal and state securities, certificates of deposit, commercial bank time deposits, savings and loan accounts and NOW accounts. They are not able to invest in district and municipal securities or repurchase agreements. The state does not require investment securities to be secured by collateral. However, there must be adequate cash flow to meet current expenses. There are no other limitations. Pooling of accounts is allowed to facilitate larger investment amounts, but records must be kept to track investments.

    School districts in Wyoming are able to borrow monies through the use of bond anticipation notes and tax anticipation notes. For bond anticipation notes, there is a dollar limit of the principle of the bond with a payback period of three years. For tax anticipation notes, there is a dollar limit of current new tax levies, and a payback limit within the current fiscal year. The proceeds of tax anticipation notes cannot be reinvested since these are warrants issued directly to creditors.

    The school districts of Wyoming are able to develop depository relationships with commercial banks and savings and loan banks. However, they cannot develop or use a limited number of banking services including safety deposit boxes, payroll disbursement, direct deposit of payroll and telephone and wire transfers and other investment services.

SECTION IV

ANNOTATED BIBLIOGRAPHY

THIS annotated bibliography contains a collection of citations of papers, articles, monographs and dissertations in the areas of school district investment, borrowing and banking written in the past 20 years. Where available, a brief description of the contents of the article or book is given, along with the number of pages. This bibliography will be useful for readers who wish to obtain more in-depth knowledge of school district financial management operations.

Papers, Monographs, Articles

Allen, G., "Increase Your District's Treasury By Bidding the Depository Funds", School Business Affairs, July, 1981.

>Quaker Community School District achieved a 40 percent average increase on the amount of interest earned during the years of 1973 through 1979. This was done by bidding the school district's complete depository of funds on a yearly basis. A reference is provided for more information. (1 page)

Commissioner's Advisory Committee for School Business Administration, The Investment of School Funds 1976, The University of the State of New York, Albany, 1976.

>The purpose of this paper is to provide a convenient and comprehensive source of information on the investment of school funds. Topics covered are: School board policy on investments; directions on how to invest; The Cash Flow Chart; types of investments; how to wire transfer funds; arbitrage guidelines; and debt service for city school districts. (20 pages)

Comptroller General of the United States, Opportunities For Savings in Interest Cost Through Improved Letter-of-Credit Methods in Federal Grant Programs, Government Accounting Office, April, 1975.

>The letter-of-credit financing method permits a recipient of a federal grant or contract to quickly obtain federal funds in a timely manner. Benefits of the system to states and the federal government are explained. (6 pages)

Daellenbach, H. G., "Are Cash Management Optimization Models Worthwhile?", Journal of Financial and Quantitative Analysis, September, 1974.

> This paper attempts to develop upper bounds of the potential savings that can be obtained from the application of cash management optimization models. The models described are grouped into three categories: Deterministic Models; Linear Programmings Models; and Dynamic Programming Models. Cost factors are considered. A Cynamic Programming Model for cash management under certainty is contrasted with simulated costs incurred by a hypothetical treasurer using simple decision rules. Prospects of realizing these potential savings are discussed for some of the models. (19 pages)

Davidson, D. B., "Automatic Payroll Deposit System", School Business Affairs, May, 1979.

> The Automatic Payroll Deposit System in Yakima, Washington's Public School District No. 7, directly transmits each employer's salary amount for each pay period to a bank or other financial institution. (2 pages)

Dembowski, F. L., and Biros, J., A Handbook of School/Banking Relations, New York State Association For School Business Officials, February, 1981.

> A return to the efficiency movement has caused increased concern about cash management on the part of school districts. Although cash management earns school districts "hard" dollars through judicious borrowing and aggressive investing, it drives school districts and banks on a potential collision course. This handbook discusses the school/banking partnership and how the relationships may be mutually beneficial. The banking industry perspective is presented, as are the services provided by banks to school districts. Bidding for banking services is discussed and sample forms provided. A direct deposit payroll system is explained in another article. The profitability analysis process used by banks to determine compensating balance is described. A discussion of the borrowing and investment possibilities available to school districts in New York State is followed by an explanation of IRS Revenue Procedure 80-55 as it affects collateralization of public deposits. (74 pages)

Annotated Bibliography 113

      Burns, T. J., "Cash Management and School/Banking Relations", A Handbook of School/Banking Relations.

      Capital District Chapter of New York State Association For Business Officials, "Bidding Banking Services", A Handbook of State/Banking Relations.

      Dembowski, F. L., "IRS Revenue Procedure 80-55: A Crisis in School District Financial Management", A Handbook of School/Banking Relations.

      Dembowski, F. L., "School-Banking Relationships: A Look to the Future", A Handbook of School/Banking Relations.

      Fingerlakes Chapter of NYS ASBO, "Direct Payroll Deposit", A Handbook of School/Banking Relations.

      New York State School Boards Association, "Tax Collection", A Handbook of School/Banking Relations.

      New York State Education Department, "The Borrowing and Investing of Funds", A Handbook of School/Banking Relations.

Dembowski, F. L., "Alternative Methods in Evaluation of School District Cash Management Programs", Journal of Education Finance Vol. 6, Summer, 1980.

    The purposes of this article are to disclose problems in the current evaluation measures used to assess the effectiveness of school district cash management practices; and to propose two new measures for evaluating school district cash management programs. A summary discusses the applicability of these techniques and possible extensions to other areas of educational policy analysis. (16 pages)

Dembowski, F. L. and Schwartz, L., "An Integer Programming Approach to School District Financial Management", <u>Socio-Economic Planning Sciences</u>, Vol. 14, 1980.

> This article is a more detailed explanation of the mathematical formulation presented at the 1979 Conference of School Business Officials. (See: Dembowski, "A Model for Determining School District Cash Flow Needs.") Several constraints are examined more fully in relation to the model: the cash balance constraint; the arbitrage model; limit on borrowing with outstanding investments; the term structure of interest rates; and borrowing period. Borrowing is included in this model making it is not only more comprehensive, but also changing it to an integer programming one. A test of this model on actual data from business managers is cited. (6 pages)

Dembowski, F. L., "An Inventory-Theoretic Techniques in School District Cash Management", <u>Educational Administration Quarterly</u>, Winter, 1981.

> Working capital management is an important aspect of school district financial management. In this analysis, two models of cash flow management derived from inventory control theory are compared with the Heuristic Approach employed by an illustrative school district. The models offer a means for optimizing the revenue school districts receive from the investment of excess funds. The model also has the potential for reducing district costs in cash flow management. (14 pages)

Dembowski, F. L., "School-Banking Relationships", <u>Educational Economics</u>, October/November, 1978.

> Why do banks need schools, and how are schools charged for their services? This article is an explanation of the processes used by banks to determine compensating cash balance requirements and annual fees. It also outlines options and additional banking services that are available to school districts. (3 pages)

Dembowski, F. L., "The Effect of the Minimum Compensating Cash Balance on School District Investments", Journal of Education Finance, Winter, 1979.

> School districts are limited in the amount of money they can invest by the compensating balance requirement of their depository bank. Banks use a profitability analysis of the checking account to set this balance. This study investigated the profitability determination of a selected school district account, and then incorporated it into a computer simulation of the cash management behavior of a district using the Miller-Orr Cash Management Model. The simulation was used to determine the optimal and fee structure for the district to negotiate with the depository bank. The study concludes that business managers should keep a $0 minimum compensating cash balance in their checking accounts and negotiate an annual fee as compensation to the bank for its services. (6 pages)

Dembowski, F. L., "Use Your Cash Management Potential", Educational Economics, July/August, 1978.

> In this article, the author advocates techniques for sound cash management. Steps are listed for accomplishment of the process of cash analysis. Opportunities are described which many school districts leave unexplored.

Hearne, J. W., "Managing Your Investment Program", School Business Affairs, February, 1980.

> A well designed investment program can help administrators get the most out of public dollars and other available resources. (2 pages)

Igner, J. E., "How to Increase Your School's Income", American School and University, May, 1979.

> Educational institutions can't let surplus cash sit idly in their checking accounts. Investments must be made and updated regularly to gain the maximum income possible. Steps for the beginning investor are outlined clearly. (5 pages)

Lawson, S., "Choosing a Bank Depository Based on Services to be Rendered to a School District", School Business Affairs, February 1980.

    School districts effect considerable savings by obtaining maximum banking services. A procedure is offered for choosing a bank depository based on services to be rendered. (2 pages)

Littman, G., "Cash Flow Planning", School Business Affairs, February, 1979.

    Cash flow statements must be well prepared to assist a school in obtaining bank credit. Expanded financial reporting (full disclosure) requires a report of essential facts which includes cash flow information. Cautions and incentives for careful determination of cash budget are explained.

Maldonado, R. M., and Ritter, L. S., "Optimal Municipal Cash Management: A Case Study", The Review of Economics and Statistics, November, 1971.

    This article illustrates the untapped potential of cash management techniques by applying them to the case of one of the better financially managed municipalities, the city and county of Honolulu. Part I presents actual cash flows of funds and cash balances for the fiscal year 1969. Parts II through IV apply three widely-known cash management models to the data, and summarizing data and presents conclusions. (4 pages)

Pogue, G. A., and Bussard, R. N., "A Linear Programming Model For Short-Term Financial Planning Under Uncertainty", Sloan Management Review, Spring, 1972.

    This paper is a valuable contribution to the literature on financial planning. The short-term financial planning problem under certainty has never before been successfully formulated as an optimization model. The authors not only do this but also apply their model to a sample problem to illustrate its use in practice. (28 pages)

Annotated Bibliography 117

Rosenberry, D. N., "Tax and Revenue Anticipation Borrowing: Discussion outline", Association of School Business Officials of the United States and Canada, Denver, Colorado, 1979.

    This is a summary of a discussion group held at the conference. It references federal law, arbitrage regulations and borrowing procedures in a series of appendices. (20 pages)

Stone, B. K., "The Use of Forecasts and Smoothing in Control - Limit Models For Cash Management", *Financial Management*, Spring, 1972.

    Real-world cash flows are neither certain, uniform and continuous nor are they completely unpredictable. There is always uncertainty in forecasting. This article formulates a control-limit inventory model of cash management that incorporates imperfect forecasts and employs simple rules to take advantage of the information contained in the cash forecasts. (12 pages)

Dissertations

Anderson, B. D., "A Study of the Investment of Idle Funds By Large Public School Systems", University of Tennessee, 1968.

Carr, M. I., "An Analysis of the Distribution of Intergovernmental Transfers of Monies and of the Investment of Idle Monies in the Public Schools of Kentucky", Indiana University, 1971.

Lykins, R. G., "A Study of Cash Management at Ohio University", Ohio University, 1971.

Meulder, W. R., "The Investment of Public School Monies", University of Southern California, 1952.

Sumner, S., "School Business Management: The Determinants of Rates of Return on the Investment of Idle Funds in New York State", Columbia University, 1974.

Welliver, W. A., "An Analysis of the Investment and Related Financial Management Practices of Pennsylvania School Districts", Temple University, 1974.

Wynn, E. L., "The Investment of Idle Monies by Georgia School Districts", University of Georgia, 1973.

FOR THOSE interested in the general management research related to these topics and referenced in some of these articles, the following list is provided.

Aronson, J. R., "The Idle Cash Balances of State and Local Governments: An Economic Problem of National Concern", Journal of Finance, June, 1968.

Baumol, W. J., "The Transactions Demand For Cash: An Inventory Theoretic Approach, The Quarterly Journal of Economics, Vol. 66, 1952.

Hausman, W., and Sanchez-Bell, A., "The Stochastic Cash Balance With Average Compensating Balance Requirements", Management Sciences, Vol. 21, April, 1975.

Miller, M. H., and Orr, D. J., "A Model For the Demand For Money By Firms", Quarterly Journal of Economics, Vol. 80, August, 1966.

Miller, M. H., and Orr, D. J., "The Demand For Money By Firms: An Extension of the Analytical Results", Journal of Finance, Vol. 23, December, 1968.

Tobin, J., "The Interest Elasticity of Transactions Demand For Cash", Review of Economics and Statistics, Vol. 38, August, 1958.

APPENDIX A ——————————————————————————————————— 119

Sample Questionnaire

SCHOOL DISTRICT CASH MANAGEMENT

A Project Sponsored by the Association of School Business Officials
of the United States and Canada

Purpose: This questionnaire is intended to compile information regarding school district borrowing, investing, and banking relations in your state. The purpose of each question is explained at the beginning of the appropriate section. The primary focus of this questionnaire is on the statutes, regulations, and opinions that authorize and delimit the cash management practices in your state. Specifically, we are interested in what cash management practices school districts can and cannot engage in by law. To this end, we ask you to not only respond to the following questions, but also to note the specific statute and section of your state's law that pertains to each question. Please add any comments you feel are necessary for clarification. If your state has a compiled list of the statutes and regulations concerning borrowing and investing, could you please send us a copy?

In Section 1, please list your name, address, and phone number so that we can contact you to verify our interpretation of your responses, and to answer any additional questions we may have. You may count on receiving the results of this project. Please return this completed questionnaire by May 15, 1981 to Dr. Fred Dembowski, ED 343, SUNY-Albany, 1400 Washington Avenue, Albany, New York 12222.

Please phone (518) 457-4058, if you have any questions regarding this questionnaire.

_____
_____

Section I. General Information

    1) Name of state_____.

    2) Name & title of respondent_____.

    3) Address of respondent _____
                                _____.

    4) Phone number of respondent (___)_____.

Section II (continued)

Other restrictions and/or limitations?

2) Which of the following securities may be used for investments?

Fund	Federal Securities	State Securities	District & Municipal Securities	Statute
a. General	___	___	___	___
b. School store	___	___	___	___
c. School lunch	___	___	___	___
d. Special aid	___	___	___	___
e. Debt service	___	___	___	___
f. Capital projects	___	___	___	___
g. Trust and agency	___	___	___	___
h. Public library	___	___	___	___
i. Bond proceeds	___	___	___	___
j. Reserves	___	___	___	___
k. Other (please list)	___	___	___	___
_____	___	___	___	___
_____	___	___	___	___
_____	___	___	___	___

3. Which of the following bank obligations may be utilized?

Fund	Repurchase Agreements	Certificates of Deposit	Commercial Bank Time Deposits	Savings & Loan Bank Time Deposits	NOW Account
a. General	___	___	___	___	___
b. School store	___	___	___	___	___
c. School lunch	___	___	___	___	___
d. Special aid	___	___	___	___	___
e. Debt service	___	___	___	___	___
f. Capital projects	___	___	___	___	___
g. Trust and agency	___	___	___	___	___
h. Public library	___	___	___	___	___
i. Bond proceeds	___	___	___	___	___
j. Reserves	___	___	___	___	___
k. Other (please list)	___	___	___	___	___
_____	___	___	___	___	___
_____	___	___	___	___	___

Restrictions and/or limitations?

Appendix A   121

Section I (continued)

   5) Which of the following govern school district financial operations in
      your state: Check all applicable.

                                              Check   Please list the
                                              Here   Principal Sections
                                              _____   _____

      Education Law   _____   _____
      Municipal Law   _____   _____
      County Law   _____   _____
      Local Finance Law   _____   _____
      Chief State School Officer's
        Regulations   _____   _____
      Comptroller's and Auditor's
        Regulations and/or opinions   _____   _____
      Other (please list)   _____   _____

      _____   _____   _____
      _____   _____   _____

   6) Number of districts in your state _____.

   7) Total interest earnings of school districts in the state for the 1979-
      1980 school year? _____.(Please estimate
      if actual earnings is not available.) _____.

Section II. School District Investing

This section is intended to obtain information concerning which investing
processes and instruments school districts can and cannot use. Besides
answering the specific questions, please list the relevant statutes, regulations, etc. that prevail in each question that were not listed previously.
If there is insufficient space to answer these questions, please use additional sheets.

   1) Which of the following sources of funds can and cannot be invested?

              Fund   Can   Cannot   Statute
              ____   ___   _____   _____

      a. General   ___   _____   _____
      b. School store   ___   _____   _____
      c. School lunch   ___   _____   _____
      d. Special aid   ___   _____   _____
      e. Debt Service   ___   _____   _____
      f. Capital projects   ___   _____   _____
      g. Trust and agency   ___   _____   _____
      h. Public library   ___   _____   _____
      i. Bond procees   ___   _____   _____
      j. Reserves   ___   _____   _____
      k. Other (please list)   ___   _____   _____

      _____   ___   _____   _____

Are there any other securities besides those listed in question 2 and 3 which may be used for school district investments? If so, please <u>list</u> and briefly explain their use.

4) Does your state require investment securities to be secured by collateral?
       Yes ___   No ____   Statute _____
If yes, please explain the collateral requirements.

5) Are there limitations as to the length and/or amounts of investments? (i.e. fiscal year, 2 years, etc.)

6) Is "pooling" of accounts allowed to facilitate larger investment amounts?

7) Can school districs invest with other districts or local government agencies?
_____Explain

8) Do you feel that any aspect of your state's investment regulations is unique or not covered above? If so, please explain.

Appendix A

Section III. School District Borrowing

This section is intended to obtain information concerning the borrowing processes and instruments that school districts can and cannot use. Again, please list the relevant statutes and regulations not previously listed and comment on unique aspects.

1) Which of the following obligations are available to school districts for short term borrowing?

Instrument	Can Use	Cannot Use	Statutes
a. Bond anticipation notes	___	___	_____
b. Budget notes	___	___	_____
c. Capital notes	___	___	_____
d. Revenue anticipation notes	___	___	_____
e. Tax anticipation notes	___	___	_____
f. Other (please list)	___	___	_____
_____	___	___	_____
_____	___	___	_____

2) What are the time and amount limitations for the borrowing obligations?

Instrument	Dollar limit	Pay back
a. Bond anticipation notes	_____	_____
b. Budget notes	_____	_____
c. Capital notes	_____	_____
d. Revenue anticipation notes	_____	_____
e. Tax anticipation notes	_____	_____
f. Other (please list)	_____	_____
_____	_____	_____
_____	_____	_____

3) Can the proceeds of the above borrowing obligations be reinvested until needed. If so, which ones can be and what are the limitations?

4) Does your state have limitations or arbitrage opportunities? If yes, please explain.

5) Are there any other aspects of short term borrowing that are important in your state that has not been covered above? If so, please explain.

Section IV. Banking Relations

This section is intended to disclose what kinds of banking relations are permitted in your state.

1) Which of the following kinds of financial institutions can the districts in your state utilize?

		Can Use	Cannot Use	Statute
a.	Commercial banks	___	___	___
b.	Saving & loan banks	___	___	___
c.	Investment firms	___	___	___
d.	Private brokers	___	___	___
e.	Other (please list)	___	___	___

2) Can districts in your state use an out-of-state bank for borrowing and/or investment purposes? If yes, please discuss limitations.

3) Which of the following banking services may be used by school districts in your state?

		Can Use	Cannot Use	Statute
a.	Tax collection	___	___	___
b.	Lock boxes	___	___	___
c.	Safety deposit boxes	___	___	___
d.	Payroll disbursement	___	___	___
e.	Check reconciliation	___	___	___
f.	Accounting and auditing	___	___	___
g.	Direct deposit of payroll	___	___	___
h.	Telephone and/or wire transfers of funds	___	___	___
i.	Handling of coin and currency	___	___	___
j.	Investment services	___	___	___
k.	Other (please list)	___	___	___

4) Are there any other limitations in school/banking relations in your state not listed previously?